The Big Idea

Should We All Be Vegan?

The Big Idea

Molly Watson

Should We All Be Vegan?

A primer for the 21st century

Over 180 illustrations

Thames & Hudson

General Editor:
Matthew Taylor

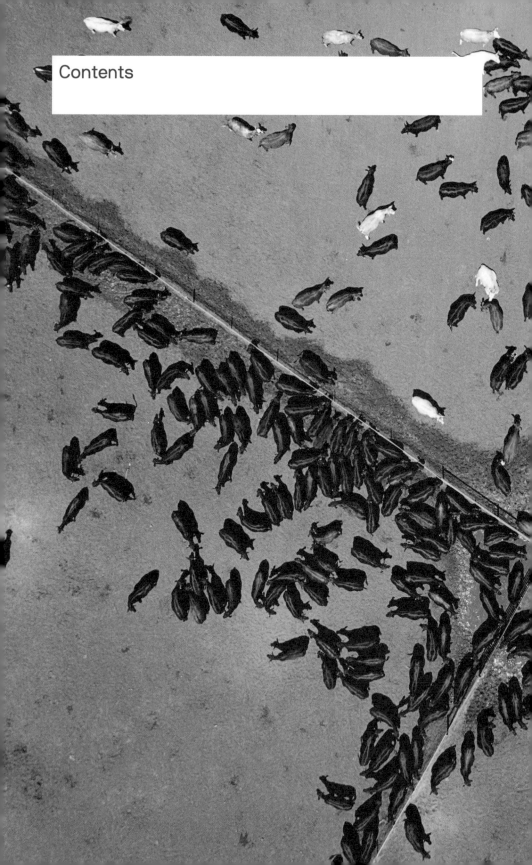

Contents

Introduction

Food trends come and go, but veganism steadily gained adherents for decades before an explosion in popularity in the 21st century. So, is a vegan diet the answer to personal and environmental health? Can humans be truly healthy on an exclusively vegan diet? What would a vegan planet look like?

A   PETA activists perform a mock execution in London on Vegan World Day, 2016. By treating a human in the same way as an animal in a slaughterhouse, they seek to highlight the barbarity of killing and eating animals.

B   This plant-based food pyramid shows how whole foods – fresh fruits and vegetables, whole grains, legumes, nuts, seeds and oils – can be eaten in proportion for a healthful and nutritious vegan diet.

The answers to such questions have a profound effect on what we eat, how we grow it and on human and environmental health.

Veganism is a diet that is free of animal products. Full stop. Vegans do not eat meat, fish, dairy, eggs or any other animal product. The difference between a vegan and a vegetarian is that vegetarians often eat eggs, dairy or both because animals are not killed to produce these foods. Vegetarians, as a rule, eat honey and other animal products, such as whey, that are derived from animals without killing them. Some people call themselves vegetarians even though they eat fish and seafood, but most vegetarians and vegans would label this diet pescatarian instead. There are also self-proclaimed flexitarians who limit how often or when they eat meat, together with people who are simply cutting down on their meat consumption in favour of plant-based foods.

For those used to Western pattern diets, a vegan diet can seem restrictive. If someone adopts veganism and simply cuts out animal products and increases the other foods they already eat, their diet may well be uninspiring. However, a well-considered vegan diet can be full of all kinds of tasty plant-based foods.

Western pattern diets emphasize meat and other animal products, including dairy, as well as root vegetables, refined grains and sweets. They do not tend to meet nutrition goals of at least five servings of fruit and vegetables per day or fibre intake, and they overshoot the mark on protein, saturated fat and sugar.

Plant-based foods are any food that comes from plants: fruits, vegetables, grains, legumes, nuts, seeds and herbs. The category includes foods that are not processed at all, such as a carrot or a head of lettuce, as well as foods that are made from plants, such as tofu, olive oil and flour.

B

Fats and oils
(use sparingly)

Leafy greens
(2–3 servings daily)

Breads
(5 servings daily)

Fruit
(3–4 servings daily)

Fats and oils
(use sparingly)

Legumes
(2–3 servings daily

Grains
(5 servings daily)

Vegetables
(unlimited amount daily)

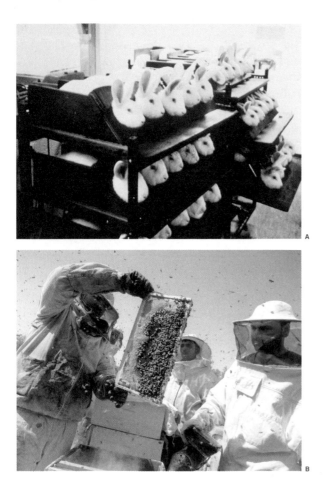

A Rabbits are strapped down in stocks during eye irritancy tests for cosmetics. Since 1998, animals can no longer be used for testing cosmetics in Britain after firms agreed to surrender their licences voluntarily. Similarly, the EU banned such testing in 2013.

B Beekeepers remove frames from a beehive to inspect the bees, assess the development of honeycomb and check for mites or other pests that can invade hives. Such routine inspections can lead to the accidental killing of bees in the hive or on the frame.

C The restaurant trend of letting customers assemble their own meal – be it a stir-fry, grain bowl or platter – is an ideal opportunity for people to experiment with combinations of vibrant produce, grains and legumes that form the base of most vegan meals.

Vegan diets are as varied as vegans themselves. A vegan breakfast could consist of oatmeal, fruit and nuts or avocado toast sprinkled with sesame seeds and extra virgin olive oil. For lunch, vegans can tuck into a wrap filled with grilled and fresh vegetables or a bowl of chilli packed with grains, beans and root vegetables. Vegan dinners can run the gamut from quinoa with sautéed veggies, roasted chickpeas and an herb sauce to saffron cauliflower rice, marinated tofu and a chopped salad. And for dessert, vegans can enjoy fruit granitas with coconut milk ice cream or cocoa chia pudding.

In short, vegan meals draw from a wide range of fruits, vegetables, grains, legumes, herbs, spices, nuts and seeds. These ingredients can be mixed and matched in endless nutritious and flavourful combinations.

Some vegans take their diets a step further into a lifestyle that shuns all animal products. For them, veganism is about freeing animals from any and all exploitation by humans, no matter how seemingly benign. It is common among vegans and even vegetarians not to wear fur or leather since animals must be killed for those products. Some vegans also avoid wearing or using silk (from silkworms) or wool (from sheep) and seek out vegan cosmetics. They do not use horsehair brushes or buy natural sponges.

The myriad of reasons for being vegan fall into three main categories: ethical, ecological and personal health.

First, many vegans believe that it is morally wrong to kill animals. The move from vegetarianism, which advocates the same thing, to veganism comes from the question of whether it is ethical to exploit animals for human gain.

One such example is honey, which strict vegans do not eat. Although bees are not killed for their honey, they make honey for their winter food. When beekeepers collect the honey, they do not always leave enough for the bees. They then supplement the hives' stores with sugar water, which is a far inferior food source for bees. Vegans believe that honey, beeswax and royal jelly are exclusively for the benefit of bees and that it is exploitative and wrong to take them.

Legumes, also known as pulses, are the seeds or pods of leguminous plants such as peas and beans. Legumes include haricot beans, green peas, soybeans, peanuts and lentils.

Vegan cosmetics are not tested or developed on animals. They do not contain any ingredients that come from animals, such as lanolin, honey, beeswax, collagen, albumen, carmine, cholesterol, gelatin, keratin or shellac.

c

A

Many vegans ask moral and ethical questions about raising animals for human use because industrial methods of animal husbandry keep animals in confined spaces, without the ability to exhibit natural behaviours. A common moral stance is that modern factory farming and industrial animal husbandry are so exploitative to both animals and the environment as to be unethical – not to mention unsustainable environmentally, socially and economically.

Second, some vegans are primarily motivated by ecological and sustainability concerns.

A   This aerial view of a Nebraska feedlot illustrates the sheer mass of animals being moved through and the complete lack of grass or other natural environment for the cattle.

B   Cattle at a feedlot in Illinois are herded inside for testing. The ultrasounds will reveal the animals' fat content and marbling – the fat running through the muscle tissue – which are key indicators of being ready for slaughter and final meat quality.

Factory farming is resource intensive, requiring greater resources per calorie than plants. Any animal raised to feed humans requires food, water and labour. Beef from feedlots, for example, takes up to 5.5 kilograms (12 lb) of grain (more than 18,000 calories) and almost 70,000 litres (18,000 gal) of water – plus energy and human labour – to produce just half a kilogram (1 lb) of beef, which offers just 1,137 calories for humans to eat. Factory farming also creates huge amounts of waste products that are harmful to the environment, including animal waste and pesticides used to grow the crops for feed.

B

On a planet with an expanding population, it is worth noting that more people can be fed with fewer resources on a plant-based diet.

Third, many people adopt a vegan diet for personal health reasons, and plenty of studies support this position.

Following a vegan diet is a clear and effective way to reduce cholesterol and saturated fats, as well as to increase anti-oxidants in a diet. People also report improved energy, clearer skin and better digestion as a consequence of eating vegan.

Industrial methods of animal husbandry include what are known as intensive farming operations in Britain and concentrated feeding operations in the USA. Both methods hold large numbers of animals in highly crowded conditions.

Natural behaviours are those that animals are driven to do and that are key to their overall health, such as chickens roosting to sleep or hogs rooting for food. An inability to express natural behaviours causes stress and even self-harm.

Feedlots are where cattle are taken to be fattened up for slaughter. In general, calves are weaned from their mothers, grazed on grassland and then transported to feedlots, where they are 'finished' by being fed grain-based feed to force them to gain weight.

A

B

In addition, veganism gets touted as a way to lose weight. Although a vegan diet does not necessarily lead to weight loss – plenty of snack foods and carbonated drinks are vegan, after all – many people report losing weight after becoming a vegan. A 2016 study published in the *Journal of General Internal Medicine* found that a vegan diet led to more short-term weight loss than a dozen other diet plans.

Foodways are the cultural, economic and social practices connected to the production and consumption of food, including traditions, regional differences, ingredients and culinary techniques.

A   Walt Disney and his family, poolside in Los Angeles, California, illustrate the rise of the hamburger as standard American fare.
B   A typical mid 20th-century dinner table, where meat – preferably a big roast – is the star of the meal.

For all those pros, there are also cons posed by veganism. Eating enough of the nutrients that are found in concentrated amounts in animal sources is the first hurdle. Social and cultural challenges accompany the nutritional ones. Following a diet that precludes animal products can make eating out stressful. Moving away from the traditional norm of a plate with meat at the centre requires adopting a whole new attitude to preparing meals, especially for the whole family. Finally, craving specific foods is also a problem for a number of people who try veganism.

The expense of maintaining a varied and healthy vegan diet can be considerable, and for some there is also an increased effort involved in meal planning and cooking. Indeed, the challenges of going and staying vegan are so significant that more than four out of five vegans and vegetarians return to eating meat and other animal products within a year. Less obvious are the problems that veganism can pose on traditional foodways, as the demand for nutrient-rich foods rises and leads to the exploitation of developing economies at the hand of Western food trends.

This book looks into all of this and more. Chapter 1 explores the history of why people have turned to animal-free diets. Chapter 2 lays out in more detail the reasons people today become vegan. Chapter 3 outlines the specific challenges people face eating vegan. Chapter 4 imagines what a vegan planet might look like ecologically, economically and culturally. The conclusion grapples with the difference between an unattainable theoretical perfect and an actionable beneficial good.

Spoiler alert: the cons of being vegan are largely those of personal inconvenience while the benefits are global and ample. It therefore begs the question: should we all be vegan? Is such a radical shift truly desirable? Is it reasonable? Is it necessary?

1. The Evolution of Veganism

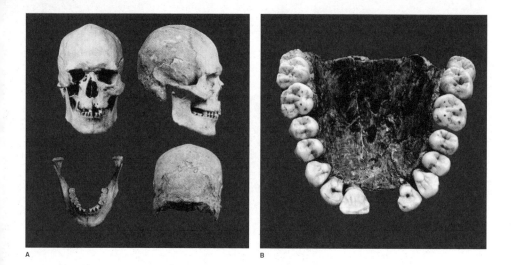

A

B

While the word 'vegan' dates from 1944 and the term 'vegetarian' was coined only about a century before that (more on both later), the practice of not eating animal products dates back to pre-historic times.

Biologically, humans are omnivores and it has served us well. Anthropologists believe we started eating meat about 2.6 million years ago – more than 2 million years before we started cooking. Eating calorie- and nutrient-dense meat may have made our brain growth possible and thus played a part in making us human.

The ability to eat a wide variety of foods means we can survive in many different environments and climates: from a fish-intensive diet in the Arctic to one featuring plenty of peanuts and yams in areas of West Africa. Humans have lived and even thrived on an incredible range of foodstuffs.

Omnivores are animals that can eat both plants and meat, as opposed to herbivores that eat only plants and carnivores that eat only meat.

As omnivores, humans were able to subsist through lean times when only a few types of food were available. In cooler climates with shorter growing seasons, food in winter could be sparse. Depending on how long slaughtered animals lasted or how successful hunting expeditions were, there could be stretches during which people adopted a vegetarian diet, and even a vegan one, out of necessity. Because humans can eat, digest and subsist on such an extensive range of foods, we have survived through full-on famines. Seaweed, bitter greens and acorns might not seem particularly appealing as foodstuffs, but they have kept people alive during tough times.

A   Human skulls can help anthropologists determine how our ancestors lived, including what they ate.

B   Teeth – particularly molars – show that humans evolved to chew and thus consume a huge variety of foods, a physical trait that has allowed us to live in a range of places.

C   Humans around the globe thrive on foods as varied as seal liver in Greenland, foraged tropical fruit in Bolivia, honeycomb in Tanzania and yak milk in Afghanistan.

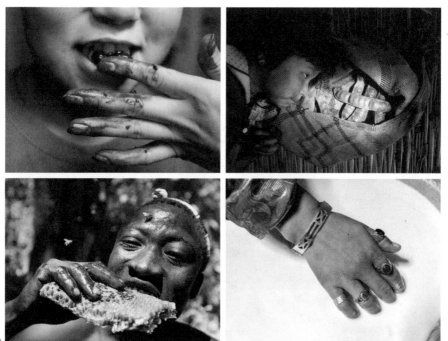

C

Not eating animals by choice though is quite a different thing, with a specific history relating to knowledge and civilization. The first known declarations of what we now call 'veganism' came from Pythagoras in ancient Greece around 500 BC. Widely lauded as 'the first vegetarian', Pythagoras was a raw food vegan, eating only uncooked – what he called 'unfired' – plant-based foods. Before the term 'vegetarian' was coined in the 1800s, a meatless diet was known in the West as a Pythagorean diet.

A

Pythagoras of Samos (*c.* 570–*c.* 495 BC) was an Ionian Greek philosopher. He is most famous for the equation $a^2 \times b^2 = c^2$, or the Pythagorean theorem for finding the area of a right angle triangle.

Socrates (*c.* 470–399 BC) is considered to be the founder of moral philosophy. His method of teaching by asking questions has been highly influential in Western thought.

A This 16th-century watercolour is titled *Do Not Eat Beans*. Pythagoras ate neither meat nor beans. Theories posit that he believed there was a connection – through reincarnation – between plants and humans.
B These figurines depict food preparation in ancient Greece: kneading bread and grating cheese. Poor people often went without meat for long stretches and the bulk of calories came from bread, but even for the poor, milk and cheese, as well as seafood, played an important role in daily diets. Pythagoras's choice to eschew all animal products was a radical one at this time.

B

Pythagoras required students who wanted to study with him to fast for 40 days before taking up his raw animal-free diet. 'As long as man continues to be the ruthless destroyer of lower living beings, he will never know health or peace,' he reasoned. 'For as long as men massacre animals, they will kill each other. Indeed, he who sows the seeds of murder and pain cannot reap joy and love.' Pythagoras was clearly a vegan on moral and ethical grounds. He also believed in metempsychosis, or reincarnation, wherein souls return in different forms after the creature dies. Part of his decision not to eat animal flesh came from believing that animals have souls, and that these souls perhaps once belonged to people.

Pythagoras was not alone. Other Greek philosophers weighed the benefit of eating animals against the harm it caused. During the next century, Plato, Socrates and Aristotle all believed that while the world existed for human use, it was a more ideal state not to kill and eat animals. As Socrates noted: 'If we pursue our habit of eating animals, and if our neighbour follows a similar path, will we not have need to go to war against our neighbour to secure greater pasturage, because ours will not be enough to sustain us, and our neighbour will have a similar need to wage war on us for the same reason?'

A For Cambodian Buddhist monks, veganism is part of their ascetic approach to eating. This also includes only eating between dawn and noon.

B The *Tacuinum Sanitatis* is a 14th-century guide that sets out six essential elements for healthy living, including the importance of a balanced diet. However, there is little evidence of purposeful animal-free diets in medieval Europe, where the rich indulged in a lot of meat while the poor – not legally able to hunt – tended to have plant-centric diets.

Around the same era, Gautama Buddha, also known as Siddhārtha Gautama, Shakyamuni Buddha or simply Buddha, lived and spread his philosophy in India. Many of his followers understand his teaching to include prohibiting eating meat. Others claim that he saw a difference between direct and indirect killing, pointing out that even those who strictly avoid all food from animals engage in indirect killing simply by walking on the ground or tilling the soil. Whichever way his words are interpreted, many of his followers have adopted meat-free or animal-free diets as way to honour his precept not to kill.

Vegetarianism is encouraged but not mandated by Hinduism. By contrast, Jainism requires vegetarianism of its adherents. Like Hinduism, Taoism holds that a vegetarian diet is ideal because it decreases suffering, but avoiding meat is not mandatory. Taoist monks are vegetarian and often follow a vegan diet that is also local and seasonal, believing that eating in harmony with nature is healthy and calming for the spirit.

Buddha (c. 563/480–c. 483/400 BC) was a philosopher or sage whose teachings became the foundation of Buddhism. Buddhists believe in the reincarnation of sentient beings and in karma as the law of moral causation.

Hinduism is widely practised in India and parts of Southeast Asia. It has numerous denominations and many ways to practise or observe it, all of which emphasize the duties of honesty, patience, forbearance, self-restraint, compassion and refraining from injuring living beings.

Jainism is an ancient Indian religion known for its asceticism, including no injury to any living creature.

Taoism, also known as Daoism, is a Chinese philosophy and belief system centred on humility and living in balance. It is based on the writings of Lao Tzu from the 6th century BC.

Although vegetarian beliefs and practices were well established in many parts of Asia by c. 500 BC, the foothold that animal-free diets had enjoyed thanks to Pythagoras and his followers took a hit during the Roman Empire. Small sects here and there shunned meat by choice, and prominent thinkers such as Seneca and Ovid claimed to be 'Pythagoreans', but vegetarianism was not popular as a philosophy, diet or lifestyle. Some people pursued a meat- or even animal free diet in the Middle Ages, but this was likely the result of being too poor to afford meat, not a philosophical position. This remained true in the West for centuries.

Spanus. oplo. ca. 7. hu. mp. Electo recen-o cui sunt rechiant ao cerel. unuinun dom incovm. 7 apunt o plia ncot. fleuninun necet uillis fice Reuid noct p̄ q̄ eluten fut comedantur cum min aut aceto. Quic gŭant nutruinum bonum. Conuehunt. frio-7 fic. sedb7 recemptnb̄.i uere 7 unregiomb; inquib; rep amen

Darhuiac comple. cali m. Ebūiaunf. Elceno. ruice oulees 7 hremules. uunuinun ecet cunc coun 7 puceune ornum. ncuninun retard it o1gome7. Reinerb ncunin cu mici reaetenone. Quic gŭant sperma 7 sanguine. aanum hueunt fr̄o 7 billis scbb7 reme 7 omnib1 regionib7.

B

Even the ultimate Renaissance man Leonardo da Vinci (1452–1519), who is well known to have been a strict non-meat eater who avoided all animal products, is an inconclusive case. Some quotes ascribed to da Vinci to prove his animal-free diet are either not from him or have been taken out of context. For a man who wrote so much about a great many topics, he recorded precious little about his personal life or habits, so drawing any conclusions is problematic.

One thing is clear, though: da Vinci thought through the implications of eating animals and considered the possibility that if humans ruled over other animals, they should grant them mercy. His logic was not widely embraced during his lifetime, but engendered more interest during the Enlightenment in the 1600s and 1700s. Enlightenment thinking challenged preconceived notions and venerated observations of the natural world. John Locke, although a meat eater, asserted that animals were capable of feeling pain and of communicating, perhaps even of feeling emotion, and that purposefully harming them was wrong. He believed if youth were allowed to torture or kill animals as a sport or for fun, it would 'harden their minds even towards men'.

A

THE
ENGLISH HERMITE,
OR,
Wonder of this AGE.

Being a relation of the life of ROGER CRAB, living neer Uxbridg, taken from his own mouth, shewing his strange reserved and unparallel'd kind of life, who counteth it a sin against his body and foule to eate any sort of Flesh, Fish, or living Creature, or to drinke any Wine, Ale, or Beere. He can live with three farthings a week.

His constant food is Roots and Hearbs, as Cabbage, Turneps, Carrets, Dock-leaves, and Grasse; also Bread and Bran, without Butter or Cheese: His Cloathing is Sack-cloath.

He left the Army, and kept a Shop at CHESHAM, and hath now left off that, and sold a considerable Estate to give to the Poore, shewing his reasons from the Scripture, Mark. 10. 21. Jer. 35.

Wherefore if meate make my brother to offend, I will never eate flesh while the world stands, 1 Cor. 8. 13.

LONDON,
Printed, and are to be sold in Popf-head Alley, and at the Exchange, 1655.

A   This frontispiece from *The English Hermite* (1655) depicts Roger Crab, a haberdasher-turned-herbalist who advocated a meat-free and alcohol-free diet. At stages, he claimed to subsist on limited food combinations, such as turnips and bran or greens and parsnips.

B   The gardens at the Palace of Versailles, designed in the 17th century, show ample space allotted to fruit trees and vegetable patches, although the palace's thousands of inhabitants were far from vegan.

The **Enlightenment** emphasized scientific learning, empirical knowledge and rationality. It led to a decrease in religious and monarchical power, the rise of liberalism and democracy, and the notion of individual human rights.

John Locke (1632–1704) was an English philosopher and physician commonly known as 'the father of liberalism'. He was an influential thinker in the development of social contract theory, whichformed the basis for modern democracies and human rights.

Voltaire (1694–1778) was a French writer, philosopher and playwright famous for his wit, which he often employed against the Catholic Church. He was also an outspoken advocate for what we now know as human rights and civil liberties.

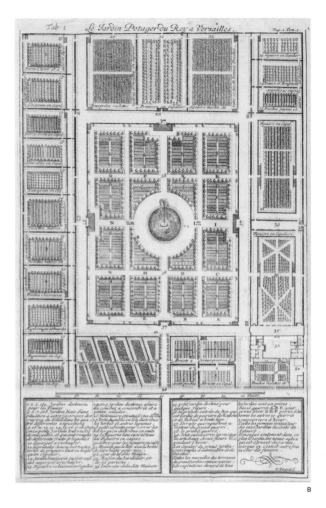

B

This viewpoint led some very prominent thinkers to turn to meat-free diets. Voltaire, for example, reportedly followed a Pythagorean diet for a time. He explored the idea that animals had feelings and suffered, and were worthy of more significant consideration than they commonly received. As he wrote in the *Philosophical Dictionary* (1764): 'How pitiful, and what poverty of mind, to have said that the animals are machines deprived of understanding and feeling.'

The admiration of nature and natural wonder displayed by English poet Alexander Pope (1688–1744) clearly played into his decision not to eat meat. Humans ruled over animals and should, therefore, be merciful. His bold, often satirical style was particularly useful when describing his abhorrence of meat eating: 'Nothing can be more shocking and horrid than one of our kitchens sprinkled with blood, and abounding with the cries of expiring victims, or with the limbs of dead animals scattered or hung up here and there. It gives one the image of a giant's den in a romance, bestrewed with scattered heads and mangled limbs.'

Even Enlightenment philosophers who did not grant that animals had much in common with humans concerning spirit or feelings, such as Immanuel Kant, often agreed that the needless killing of them was morally bad for the people who did it. He noted: 'If he is not to stifle his own feelings, he must practise kindness towards animals, for he who is cruel to animals becomes hard also in his dealings with men. We can judge the heart of a man by his treatment of animals.'

A

Immanuel Kant (1724–1804) was a German philosopher whose doctrine of transcendental idealism has been a significant influence on modern philosophy. He argued that reason is the basis of morality.

A   This portrait of 1803 depicts Joseph Ritson, an ardent promoter of a meat-free diet who believed 'the use of animal food disposed man to cruel and ferocious action'.
B   As philosophers, poets and religious communities explored a range of meat-free diets in the 19th century, the era also saw the rise of industrialized slaughterhouses, such as Besançon in France, designed for efficiency rather than the humane treatment of animals.

B

Meanwhile, across the Atlantic, Benjamin Franklin (1706–90), one of the founding fathers of the USA, also experimented with a meat-free diet. Like Voltaire, the extent of his commitment is difficult to pin down, but his admiration for the effects of living meat-free is evident. 'My refusing to eat meat occasioned inconveniency,' he wrote, 'and I have been frequently chided for my singularity. But my light repast allows for greater progress, for greater clearness of head and quicker comprehension.' Unlike Voltaire, the appeal of not eating meat seems driven by the results Franklin felt personally rather than by philosophical principles. This shows a shift in how and why people considered whether they should eat animals.

A

Enlightenment thinking used reason and rationality to question the Church and other conventional wisdom, including the morality of eating animals. In the early 1800s, the Romantics applied the same approach to reflect on personal experience, building on Franklin's assessment of how a meat-free diet made him feel.

By the time the English poet Percy Bysshe Shelley (1792–1822) wrote *A Vindication of a Natural Diet* in 1813 (remember, the term 'vegetarian' did not exist yet), he could take for granted the moral ideal of not killing a fellow creature and focus on the personal health benefits of an animal-free diet: 'There is no disease, bodily to mental, which adoption of vegetable diet and pure water has not infallibly mitigated, wherever the experiment has been fairly tried.'

His wife, Mary Wollstonecraft Shelley (1797–1851), author of *Frankenstein; or The Modern Prometheus* (1818), had a less clear relationship with plant-based eating but was rumoured to follow her husband's meat-free diet. Interestingly, she made her literary creation Dr Frankenstein's oft-misunderstood monster a herbivore. As the latter explains in the novel: 'I do not destroy the lamb and the kid to glut my appetite; acorns and berries afford me sufficient nourishment.' Mary used the creature's diet to signal his essentially peaceful nature.

Along with the Shelleys, their fellow Romantic poet Lord Byron (1788–1824) also reputedly did not eat meat. Lord Byron's decision seems to have been less connected to morality or even physical well-being than to asceticism and self-deprivation as a spiritual activity. Although he avoided meat, he apparently did not have a problem eating fish, and his extreme diet would sometimes be restricted to biscuits and water.

Romantic philosophy emphasized the importance of imagination and emotion and believed that improving the human condition rested on the self-awareness and personal experience of the individual. Romantic literature tended to focus or at least draw on autobiographical material.

A   *Album Benary* (c. 1876) is the work of Ernst Benary, a German botanist who expanded and modernized vegetable seed breeding. Just as awareness of vegetarianism increased, an immense variety of vegetables were becoming available.

B   This 18th-century Russian woodcut shows different scenarios in which the world is turned upside down. The central 'ox as butcher' is drawn from Aesop's fable, in which the oxen decide not to kill the butchers because at least they do their job skilfully with minimum suffering.

While the British Romantics experimented with meat-free diets, so too did prominent US Transcendentalists. Henry David Thoreau noted that people who thought they could not be healthy and strong without meat to build muscle and bone (a common myth at the time) had failed to consider all the large vegetarian animals, such as horses and cows. He concluded: 'I have no doubt that it is part of the destiny of the human race, in its gradual improvement, to leave off eating animals, as surely as the savage tribes have left off eating each other.'

As interest in meat-free eating grew, it got a new name: vegetarianism.

Transcendentalists followed an idealistic philosophy connected to Romanticism and Kantian philosophy. Transcendentalism asserts the primacy of individual experience, the importance of self-reliance and the divinity inherent in nature.

Henry David Thoreau (1817–62) was a US poet and philosopher best known for his book *Walden* (1854). As a leading Transcendentalist, he used the logic and empirical observation of the Enlightenment, along with the veneration of the everyday and the natural world of the Romantics, in his search for meaning and purpose.

The **Bible Christian Church**, founded in 1809, believed a meat-free diet was a form of temperance or control of one's appetite.

A

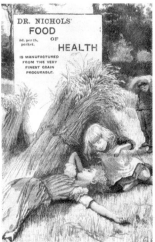

Alcott House was a cooperative spiritual community and progressive school, in what is now Greater London, that operated from 1838 to 1848. Members ate no animal products and practised celibacy.

Religious revivals occurred during the 1800s when many new Christian sects began, including the Church of Jesus Christ of Latter-day Saints and the Seventh-day Adventists. They tended to focus on the second coming of Jesus Christ and the importance of temperate behaviour. Some, but by no means all, of these groups practised varying levels of vegetarianism or veganism.

Seventh-day Adventists are a Protestant Christian denomination founded in 1863 in Michigan. They emphasize the imminent second coming of Jesus Christ and celebrate the Sabbath on Saturdays.

The word 'vegetarian' was popularized by a group of people that included members of the Bible Christian Church and Alcott House, as well as readers of *The Truth Tester* journal (a health and temperance publication), when they formed the Vegetarian Society in Ramsgate, England, in 1847. As shown by the founders of the society, meat-free eating was sometimes included in the religious revivals of the 19th century. Most famously, the Seventh-day Adventists were, and remain, proponents of vegetarianism for its health properties. While vegetarianism is not required of Seventh-day Adventists, it is commonly practised.

A   This *Punch* cartoon (1852) mocks vegetarianism with an imagining of its natural outcome. At this time, meat- or animal-free diets were a radical practice associated with progressive politics or an evangelical style of Christianity.

B   Dr Nichols's *Penny Vegetarian Cookery: The Science and the Art of Selecting and Preparing a Pure, Healthful and Sufficient Diet* (1891) features a mix of health claims and promotions of his proprietary health and hygiene products, such as soap.

A

Brothers Will Keith Kellogg (1860–1951) and John Harvey Kellogg (1852–1943), famed for inventing modern breakfast cereal, were Adventists. John Harvey was a nutritionist and health activist, who founded a sanitarium in Battle Creek, Michigan, where vegetarianism was part of the treatment, alongside enemas, exercise, sunshine and hydrotherapy. He was an ardent eugenicist, believing in the superiority of the white race and the need to further perfect it on an individual and group level. He thought that vegetarianism would help create pure blood and advocated no meat eating through the Race Betterment Foundation, which he established. Along with vegetarianism, he promoted sexual abstinence and spearheaded anti-masturbation campaigns. There is ample reason to believe that he never consummated his marriage, as he and his wife adopted seven children and fostered more than 40.

Russian writer Leo Tolstoy (1828–1910) was also a vegetarian and sought to inspire others to follow his lead. His thoughts on vegetarianism – that '[the vegetarian]

A **sanitarium** is a health resort or medical spa, not to be confused with a sanitorium, which is a medical facility for long-term care.

Eugenicists were followers of eugenics. Popular in the late 19th and early 20th centuries, eugenics was held up as scientific proof of the perfectibility of the human race. It encouraged the breeding of people with desirable traits and discouraged the reproduction of those with undesirable ones.

Mahatma Gandhi (1869–1948) was an Indian activist against British colonial rule. He famously led non-violent protests and inspired civil rights movements around the world.

Henry Stephens Salt (1851–1939) was an English writer who focused on social reform. He is widely credited with being the first person to champion the modern notion of animal rights, not just argue for animal welfare.

movement should cause special joy to those whose life lies in the effort to bring about the kingdom of God on earth ... because it is a sign that the aspiration of mankind towards moral perfection is serious and sincere' – harked back to those of ancient Greek philosophers.

Tolstoy's writing on vegetarianism as a source of human progress influenced none other than Mahatma Gandhi. The two engaged in a long correspondence on their mutual interest in non-violence and peace, with vegetarianism being part of and symbolic of both. As Gandhi said: 'I do feel that spiritual progress does demand at some stage that we should cease to kill our fellow creatures for our bodily wants.' Gandhi had first been introduced to vegetarianism as a philosophical and political stance, rather than a religious mandate, by Henry Stephens Salt, who pointed Gandhi to Thoreau's thoughts on meat eating.

A most entertaining example of rejecting meat comes from Irish playwright George Bernard Shaw (1856–1950). Removing meat from his diet started as a way to save money, but being vegetarian became part of his sense of moral and physical superiority. He wrote: 'It seems to me, looking at myself, that I am a remarkably superior person, when you compare me with other writers, journalists and dramatists; and I am perfectly content to put this down to my abstinence from meat. That is the simple and modest ground on which we should base our non-meat diet.' For Shaw, vegetarianism was about the perfection of the self.

Throughout history, not eating meat or declaring oneself vegetarian had, as it does today, a range of meanings.

The label 'strict vegetarian' often referred to someone who did not eat any animal products. Then, in 1944, Donald Watson coined the term 'vegan' as a way to differentiate between strict vegetarians and less strict ones. The goal was to come up with something more concise than 'non-dairy vegetarian'. Watson noted that a shorter name would also save time when he typed the newsletter for his group of fellow strict vegetarians, which would henceforth be known as the Vegan Society. Some other possibilities he considered included 'dairyman', 'vital' and 'benevore'.

Even with the new name, veganism did not gain much traction in broader society. While the number of self-declared vegetarians went up in Britain during World War II, this may have been because such a declaration led to greater cheese rations, which were larger and more reliable than meat ones.

Donald Watson (1910–2005) was an English animal rights activist. Growing up in Yorkshire, not eating meat was unheard of, but Watson was haunted after witnessing the slaughter of a pig on his uncle's farm and gave up meat at the age of 14. He stopped eating eggs and dairy as an adult.

During post-war rationing, engaging in a more restricted diet was not very appealing. The fact that Hitler was a vegetarian did not help the movement's image in the West either. How strict or consistent a vegetarian Hitler was remains debatable. His food taster claimed that he never ate meat during her tenure, whereas his cook before the war said he ate it regularly. In any case, his interest in vegetarianism seems to have stemmed from notions of bodily purity that were developed in the late 19th century by vegetarians such as John Harvey Kellogg.

A   In this German satirical cartoon (c. 1910), the rabbit declares: 'Now no phoney sentimentality! The principle of free research requires that I vivisect this human for the health of the entire animal world.'

B   This caricature on Goering's anti-vivisection law of 1933 appeared in the satirical journal *Kladderadatsch*. Surprising to many, the Nazi Party pushed for a range of progressive animal rights protections.

C   In *The Vegan News* (1944), Donald Watson wrote: '... we believe the spiritual destiny of man is such that in time he will view with abhorrence the idea that men once fed on the products of animals' bodies.'

c

An animal-free diet had always been a fringe practice in the West, with its practitioners often seen as outcasts. However, in the 1960s and 1970s, being on the fringe of society lost some of its stigma. Unconventional lifestyles became more common, and avoiding meat saw an increase in popularity.

New factors started to weigh in on the decision to become vegan. Moral and health considerations still mattered, but concerns about both the environment and animal welfare – and how they might be connected – arose as new reasons to avoid food derived from animals.

A

A In the 1970s, various communes, such as The Farm (pictured here and still an 'intentional community' in central Tennessee), explored the possibilities of large-scale vegetarian and vegan cooking.

B The International Society for Krishna Consciousness is a branch of Hinduism dating from 16th-century Bengal. Its followers eat a strict vegetarian diet, and many hold a vegan diet to be an even higher ideal.

B

In 1971, US author Frances Moore Lappé (b. 1944) wrote *Diet for a Small Planet*. It is still in print and has sold more than 3 million copies to date. Its popularity stems from how it connects the dots between meat production, food waste and environmental impacts, which gave a generation a new reason to assess their consumption of animal products. The moral question around the rights and wrongs of eating meat no longer only concerned personal health or individual ethics; it was about survival as a species and the health of the planet. Lappé redefined what we eat not only as a dietary or culinary act, or even a moral one as had so many vegetarians before, but also as a political one. She stressed that our diet matters not only for our health, but also for the world at large. The personal is political, as the saying goes, even in the form of a meal. In addition to showing how global hunger does not result from a lack of food, but from the inefficient distribution of resources, the book offers tips on healthy eating and simple recipes.

In 1975, Australian ethics professor Peter Singer (b. 1946) published *Animal Liberation*. His position is two-fold. He believes that people should try to reduce suffering in the most effective manner possible. Not harming, much less killing animals, is part of this because, he argues, the line between humans and animals is an arbitrary one. Humans and great apes, for example, are more alike than great apes and ants. He also argues against testing on animals in most instances and has helped to popularize the global animal rights movement, which has led to a shift away from the default testing of products on animals. His work has added a clear moral reasoning to fuel the growing interest in vegetarian and vegan diets.

When Paul McCartney announced he was a vegetarian in 1975, it further spurred interest in the practice. His wife Linda published a vegetarian cookbook in 1989 and launched a line of vegetarian foods in 1991. Sir Paul is now an outspoken vegan and promotes Meat-Free Mondays to encourage people to eat vegetarian or vegan meals once a week.

Another important touchpoint in the evolution of veganism was the documentary *The Animals Film* (1981). Co-directed by Victor Schonfeld and

A

A   Filming *The Animals Film*. The first feature documentary to offer a comprehensive examination of human exploitation of animals and to draw positive attention to animal rights activism.
B   Greenpeace built a reputation for calling out the violence of industries that exploit animals, as seen in this campaign against fur photographed by David Bailey in 1986.

Myriam Alaux, the film chronicles the exploitation of animals by humans – in farming, as pets, for entertainment, in scientific and military research – using specially shot scenes, secret government footage, cartoons, newsreels and excerpts from propaganda films. It also profiles the actions and ideas of the international animal rights movement and of the Animal Liberation Front. The film was released in cinemas in the USA, Canada, Germany, Austria, Australia and Britain to critical acclaim. Its biggest impact was in Britain when it played on Channel Four in November 1982 and on Sweden's SVT2 thereafter. It prompted many viewers to become lifelong activists for veganism.

More recently, in 2002, Michael Pollan (b. 1955) published his article 'Power Steer' in The New York Times, opening up the discussion of not only animal welfare, but the whole production system. It traces the life of a calf from birth to slaughter, and shows how animal welfare, environmental impact and nutritional concerns are all part of a single system. It also highlights the impact factory farming has on animals, our food and the environment as a whole. The article's cogent explanation of how we raise cows for our benefit, with little regard for their natural inclinations, diets or digestive systems, struck a chord with people who were becoming more interested in where their food comes from. While Pollan himself argues for a considered, ethical omnivore existence that seeks out animals raised in a better way, his investigation opened a wider debate about animal welfare and a broader conscience about how food is produced.

A

The rise of celebrities choosing veganism in the past few decades has helped fuel the mainstream adoption of a vegan diet and lifestyle.

In 1985 The Smiths' *Meat is Murder* album influenced many fans to go vegetarian. Outspoken frontman Morrissey has always championed animal rights, and became vegan in 2015. Actress Alicia Silverstone has been a vocal advocate of a vegan diet for more than a decade. The musician Moby is another famous long-time vegan activist. He explained: 'If you don't want to be beaten, imprisoned, mutilated, killed or tortured, then you shouldn't condone such behaviour towards anyone, be they human or not.'

Well-known vegans now include the likes of Mike Tyson, Ellen DeGeneres, Ellen Page, Gwen Stefani, Sinéad O'Connor and Thom Yorke.

Actress Natalie Portman actively promotes veganism, explaining that her values-based decision in terms that are not too dissimilar to how Pythagoras might have put it: 'Eating for me is how you proclaim your beliefs three times a day. That is why all religions have rules about eating. Three times a day, I remind myself that I value life and do not want to cause pain to or kill other living beings. That is why I eat the way I do.'

A   The increasing availability of vegan food extends to services such as the plant-based dishes shipped by Purple Carrot, a meal kit delivery company based in the USA, designed to help people cook vegan food at home.

B   Vegan fashion is on the rise, everything from shoes and boots to belts and bags. Items that were once made of leather, such as Dr Martens boots, are being produced using animal-free (often dubbed cruelty-free) options, including 'pleather' made of polyurethane.

A

Former vice president of the USA and environmentalist Al Gore, who wrote and narrated *An Inconvenient Truth* (2006), has been vegan since 2013, following in the footsteps of former US president Bill Clinton, who went vegan three years earlier to improve his heart health and to lose weight.

Beyond a tide of celebrities, the rising interest in plant-based foods is clear as the market for vegan foods grows around the world, including the opening of vegan restaurants and bakeries, the creation of vegan cheese and the production of vegan frozen foods. Even France, a nation famed for its meat- and cheese-eating ways, has seen the demand for vegetable proteins (tofu, seitan, etc.) increase.

The industry was worth more than $34 million in 2016 and it is expected to grow another 25% annually up to 2020.

Calculating exactly how many vegans there are is tricky. People define veganism differently, and the figures are self-reported. However, the number of people who say they are vegan is on the rise. As of 2018, 7% people in Britain defined themselves as vegan. In the USA, only 1% of the population said they were vegan in 2014. By 2017, the figure had risen to 3%, or as high as 6% depending on the poll. Veganism also has a foothold in countries such as Poland, where 7% of the population reports following a vegan diet, Israel (5%) and Sweden (4%). While these numbers represent the growing trend in the West, they have nothing on India, where a history of religious and cultural norms that eschew eating animals means that 27% of the population reports following a vegan diet.

Tofu is made by grinding and straining soybeans, coagulating the resulting 'milk' to separate the solids and liquids, and then pressing the solids into blocks.

Seitan is made from wheat protein or gluten. It has a meat-like texture along with a meat-like amount of protein.

A   Biocultura is an international trade show featuring eco and sustainable products from around the world, including an increasing amount of vegan meat substitutes.

B   Impossible Foods has created a vegan burger that 'bleeds' (top), using a yeast extract for the red tinge and a mineral flavour of beef. McDonald's introduced the McVegan (bottom) in 2017.

2. Why Go Vegan Today?

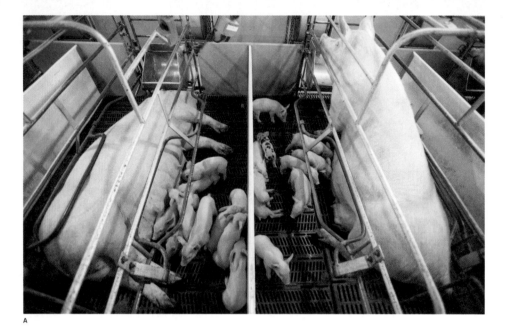

A

The reasons to become a vegan – moral, ecological and personal health – are inter-connected in compelling ways.

If someone believes meat is murder, vegetarianism is the obvious solution to their moral objection to killing animals. If someone believes exploitation of animals is wrong, veganism offers the same clear-cut escape from unethical action.

The ethical concerns about exploiting animals are greatly augmented by the manner in which most animals are raised in our current food system. Conditions are often so bad that it is easy to see why someone might decide to opt out.

B

A These breeding sows at a farm in Maryland
   are housed in a typical gestational crate.
   It is big enough for them to lie down but
   not turn around, much less demonstrate
   any of their natural behaviours such as
   rooting or burrowing.

B Chickens that are being raised for meat
   live cage-free in a chicken house, but
   the conditions are still extremely cramped,
   and indoors. Even free-range birds often
   only have limited access to the outdoors,
   which some never get to use.

Mega-farms or intensive farming and industrial slaughter-houses are part of a system that seeks efficiency and economy at all costs. Such farms, also known as concentrated animal feeding operations (CAFOs), are classed as those that raise more than 40,000 birds, 2,000 pigs or 750 breeding sows in Britain and 125,000 broiler chickens, 82,000 laying hens, 2,500 pigs, or 700 dairy or 1,000 beef cattle in the USA. The largest of these farms in Britain hold more than 1 million chickens, 23,000 pigs and 3,000 heads of cattle. The consequences are many, including abysmal animal welfare. Originating in the USA, where there were more than 19,000 such operations as of 2016, there are now over 800 livestock intensive farming operations in Britain, and nearly every county in England and Northern Ireland is home to at least one such farm. In Brazil, CAFOs are steadily replacing traditional methods of raising cattle, as the country seeks to raise more beef without continuing to create more grazing land by cutting down forests. Even in France, where farmers' unions have fought against mega-farms, large-scale dairy operations capable of milking 1,000 cows have opened. Of course, this figure is modest when compared to the 40,000-cow dairy operation in Mudanjiang, China, which was expanded in 2016 to handle 100,000 cows. According to the United Nations, CAFOs account for 72% of poultry, 42% of egg and 55% of pork production around the world.

A

Chickens, whether raised for meat (broilers) or eggs (laying hens), are routinely kept in horribly crowded conditions. Even after the improvements legislated in 2012, egg-laying hens are still commonly kept in battery cages the size of a piece of letter or A4 paper and not nearly big enough for their metre-wide wingspan. Before these improvements, such cages were sometimes as small as half this size.

Battery cages were designed to make egg-collecting easier. They also keep the birds from moving around too much and thus using energy on anything other than producing eggs.

A **debeaked** chick has had its beak cut or burnt off without an anaesthetic. The process is painful and deprives chicks of one of their primary sensory receptors.

Until 2012, all chickens in Britain were also commonly debeaked to keep them from pecking each other to death. The term 'pecking order' comes from the strict, pecking-based hierarchy within chicken flocks, which manifests itself in higher status chickens pecking lower status birds. Once the pecking order within a flock is established, the chickens tend to exist in relative peace, as long as they have ample space in which to live and enough food and water for everyone in the flock. Trouble arises when either space or food is in short supply. Birds foreign to an established flock may well be pecked to death if they cannot defend themselves. Chickens will also peck each other when stressed or frustrated, hence the debeaking. Laying hens still have their beaks clipped in Britain, as they do throughout Europe and the USA.

Broiler chickens do not fare much better. The most intensively farmed ones are kept in dimly lit sheds of up to 30,000 birds. Although not in cages, they are allotted the same small amount of space per bird. In such close confinement, disease spreads quickly, so the use of antibiotics is common.

These chickens barely resemble anything from nature. When bred to be the ultimate egg-laying and meat-producing units, they often cannot stand or walk properly even when given the space to do so.

The crowded, unhealthy conditions that are allowed in the USA mean that disease – notably salmonella – is rife, and washing the birds in chlorine to 'disinfect' them is common practice. When executed correctly, this can reduce the spread of disease, but the process is often incomplete, exposing the meat to harsh chemicals without killing all the bacteria. The practice can also reduce odour, allowing meat to 'pass' for fresh for longer. Chlorine washing is banned in the EU, which focuses on improving hygiene standards to limit the growth of bacteria in the first place.

A The industrialization of hatching and raising chickens for eggs en masse includes assembly line efficiency and factory conditions. It also involves killing all male chicks: they are gassed, suffocated or shredded/ crushed alive.

B Even the size of baby chicks has increased by almost a third since the 1950s, and the rate at which they have been bred to grow has increased some ten-fold. They have also been bred to be breast-heavy in order to meet the increased demand for white meat.

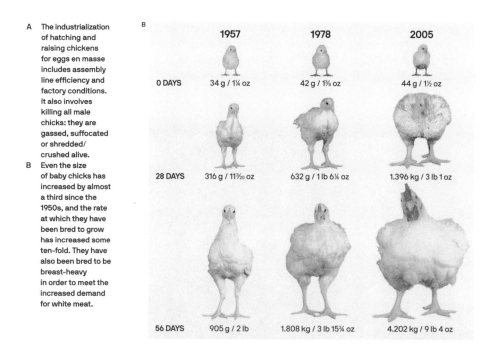

	1957	1978	2005
0 DAYS	34 g / 1¼ oz	42 g / 1⅗ oz	44 g / 1½ oz
28 DAYS	316 g / 11²⁄₂₀ oz	632 g / 1 lb 6¼ oz	1.396 kg / 3 lb 1 oz
56 DAYS	905 g / 2 lb	1.808 kg / 3 lb 15¾ oz	4.202 kg / 9 lb 4 oz

Things do not get any better with the mammals we raise.

Hogs are kept in equally torturous conditions. Breeding sows are housed in farrowing crates so small they cannot turn around, and piglets often have their teeth clipped to prevent them biting each other in the crowded conditions. The floors of the hog sheds are slatted so that the pigs' waste can drop through. These hard floors are so unnatural for pigs, which evolved to roam meadows and forests, that the animals have been bred to have tougher hooves.

Like chickens, pigs have been raised to grow bigger and faster on less feed, creating animals that cannot survive outside the industrial farming system. In some slaughterhouses, more than 1,000 hogs are stunned per hour, making a 'humane' death impossible. Some are still alive when they are lowered into the scalding tank.

A

B

A   Industrial chicken slaughter is a fast-paced business. Not every bird is necessarily dead before it gets dipped in scalding water to remove its feathers.

B   At one time, dairy cows grazed the meadows during the day but now they face industrial conditions that prohibit their natural behaviours. Some are even kept indoors, with no access to the grass their stomachs are designed to digest.

Dairy cows are treated a little better. In most places, dairy cows are kept on pasture for most of the year and housed within a reasonable space in the winter. Intensive dairy farming does exist though, in which cows are shut in milking sheds year-round. On dairy mega-farms in the USA, cows are kept in sheds and fed feed instead of grazing on pasture. This no- or low-grass diet leads to digestive problems, because, as ruminants, cows are designed to process grass, not grain. Furthermore, breeding high-yield animals can make dairy cows so productive that their udders are heavy enough to cause pain and difficulty when standing or walking.

A Animal rights activists give pigs their last drink of water as they arrive at the Farmer John slaughterhouse in Vernon, California. The activists hold these 'pig vigils' to protest the conditions, treatment and slaughter of the animals.

B On the way to the slaughterhouse, the truck floor becomes covered in waste, leaving the animals to stand in their own filth and breathe in the toxic ammonia from their uric acid.

C Butchers slaughter and break down cattle at a slaughterhouse in Nairobi, Kenya. They need to inspect the carcasses for plastic bags, banned in Kenya in 2017, which get caught in trees and bushes and ingested by animals, including livestock.

Beef cattle are raised on pasture most of their lives, but their final stop at feedlots in most countries makes them vulnerable to all the problems of crowding and disease found in other intensive farming.

Feedlots are so crowded that the plants cows naturally eat cannot grow on the packed, manure-covered dirt. Instead of grazing, beef cattle are fed to fatten them up quickly and cheaply. They are most often fed grains, often corn, along with hay or silage and some protein from soy. In some countries, including the USA, they can also be given food by-products, such as beet tops from sugar production, crumbs from baking facilities and distillers' spent grain. During the finishing stage of industrial beef production, with the exception of beef cattle that are 100% grass-fed and grass-finished, the animals are not fed anything – besides hay – that they would naturally eat by choice, no matter where they are raised.

In addition, when it comes to slaughter time, it has been shown that a large number of animals experience fear, panic and pain.

For many, even the transport to the slaughter-house is a stressful, health-risking journey. Hot prods and electric shocks are commonly used to move cattle into transport vehicles that are crowded, hot and poorly ventilated. Adequate water is often lacking. The jostling, noise and sudden movements that occur as the animals are guided along chutes and ramps cause physical stress, which has been shown to affect meat quality.

c

A

While poor conditions create physical ailments, they also prevent animals from exhibiting basic natural behaviours that bring them pleasure and promote their comfort and health. Being unable to engage in such behaviour leads to stress, aggression and often self-injury. The entire system has led to some extreme solutions: hogs cannot wallow in mud to cool down, so their sheds must be air-conditioned; chickens cannot dust bath to protect themselves from mites and lice, so pesticides are used to control them.

Behaviour distortion extends to upending how the animals relate to one another. Chickens cannot establish natural pecking orders, and so peck themselves. Dairy cows and their calves are separated soon after birth, whereas left to follow natural instincts and physical needs, a calf would not self-wean until nine to twelve months. Hogs – social animals that are smarter than dogs and just as affectionate – cannot dig hollows in which to give birth, much less raise their piglets or socialize.

The conditions are appalling for the animals, obviously, but these methods are harmful for the farm workers, too.

Exposure to vast amounts of animal waste can lead to digestive problems, possible contamination by any bacteria or viruses in the waste and to respiratory problems. Beyond exposure to waste, vaccinating or administering antibiotics and other drugs to large animal populations can result in farmers accidentally sticking themselves, and there are even reports of psychological trauma as workers have to harm the animals they care for. Many chicks and piglets in intensive farming are killed because they are sick: piglets by a blow to the head, chicks by being thrown on the ground.

A   Piglets have a high casualty rate at intensive farming operations. Some get sick; others are crushed in the crowded conditions. They are not alone: death rates for sows almost doubled between 2013 and 2016 at such farms in the USA.
B   Workers leave a Tyson chicken factory in Springdale, Arkansas, after a chlorine leak – the chlorine is used to disinfect the meat.
C   A farm worker walks the floor of an intensive chicken farming operation, clearing dead or injured birds from the flock. It is a regular task at any such farm.

The speed at which meat-processing workers are asked to operate and the sharp tools and strong chemicals used mean that they face injury at twice the national average for similar jobs. And injuries can be significant: back problems, torn muscles, pinched nerves, broken bones and deep cuts are all common.

A vegan diet is one way some people take a stance against the system of industrialized processing and its cruelty to animals and people. None of a vegan's food budget is being spent in direct support of such practices. But for people disgusted by this system, although not necessarily against farming animals in principle, perhaps the answer is to improve conditions for animals.

A

Pastured pork could be allowed to live in their natural social arrangements outside; chickens could spend their days on fields where they could hunt and peck; grass-fed beef could be used to restore overworked land with their aerating hooves and soil-enriching manure. Animals raised with such care would cost more and there would be fewer of them. However, eating less meat would, as we will see, be just fine.

The environmental fallout of industrial farming can be as horrific as its treatment of animals. It is another reason why people may choose to follow a vegan diet.

B

A

In traditional farming, animal waste is part of a 'virtuous cycle', in which manure is tilled back into the soil as a fertilizer. Ruminants aerate the soil on fields as they graze; chickens keep insects in check as they peck. This feedback loop is cut off when animals are sequestered in sheds. When animals are kept in confined and crowded conditions, they produce more waste than can be absorbed by neighbouring fields.

Some waste from intensive farming can get processed as manure, but often there is too much to deal with.

Fertilizer is used to return valuable nitrogen and carbon to the soil. Manure is particularly prized because it slowly releases nitrogen. Too much nitrogen at once can 'burn' plants.

Ponds or lagoons of hog waste spread a noxious smell far beyond the confines of the sheds, and fresh water utilized to wash out the sheds increases overall water use. Waste at beef feedlots sits on the ground, often getting washed away by rain into nearby waterways.

B

In addition to the sheer volume of waste, faeces and urine become combined in intensive farming. Urine, while full of nitrogen, potassium and other nutrients that make good fertilizer, also contains sodium. Plus, much of the nitrogen is found in concentrated amounts, meaning it must be diluted to work as an effective fertilizer. When combined with faeces, the amount of urine can make all of the waste unusable.

A/B The contents of more than 110 manure lagoons (open-air pits or literal cesspools of hog waste) at different industrial pig farms in North Carolina were flooded during Hurricane Florence in 2018. Many breached, releasing their contents into the flood waters and surrounding environment, causing widespread contamination. Past floods have shown dangerous levels of *E. coli* and *Clostridium perfringens* even after flood waters recede.

Factory farms also employ a high volume of water, which has a hugely negative impact on the environment, particularly in water-starved regions. Overall, meat uses far more water to 'grow' than other types of food, and approximately a quarter of the world's fresh water goes towards livestock each year.

Beef, the worst offender, takes as much as 15,400 litres (4,068 gal) of water to create a single kilogram (2.2 lb). A kilogram (2.2 lb) of most legumes requires around 4,000 litres (1,057 gal), although soy beans need only half that. Most fruits and vegetable are far less thirsty: apples take just 822 litres (217 gal) per kilogram (2.2 lb) of harvested fruit.

The antibiotics given to livestock do not just disappear once they are administered; they live on in the meat, in the animals' waste and in the environment.

Antibiotic resistance occurs when a bacterium becomes resistant to an antibiotic. This happens because the bacterium is exposed to but not killed by the antibiotic and then reproduces.

But antibiotic resistance is growing. Reasons for this include the over-prescription of antibiotics to humans, people taking antibiotics when they will not work (for a virus, for example) and not taking a full dose as prescribed. It can also happen when animals are given sub-therapeutic doses of antibiotics,

A

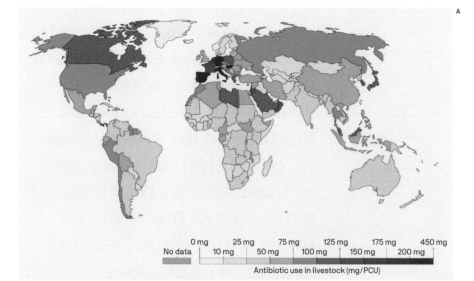

| No data | 0 mg | 25 mg | 75 mg | 125 mg | 175 mg | 450 mg |
| | 10 mg | 50 mg | 100 mg | 150 mg | 200 mg | |

Antibiotic use in livestock (mg/PCU)

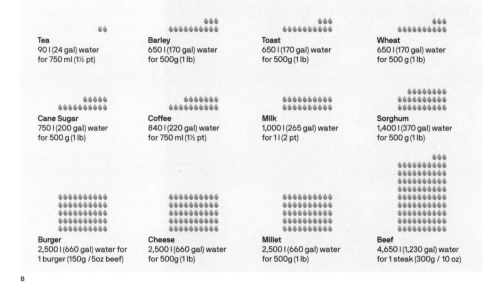

Tea
90 l (24 gal) water
for 750 ml (1½ pt)

Barley
650 l (170 gal) water
for 500g (1 lb)

Toast
650 l (170 gal) water
for 500g (1 lb)

Wheat
650 l (170 gal) water
for 500 g (1 lb)

Cane Sugar
750 l (200 gal) water
for 500 g (1 lb)

Coffee
840 l (220 gal) water
for 750 ml (1½ pt)

Milk
1,000 l (265 gal) water
for 1 l (2 pt)

Sorghum
1,400 l (370 gal) water
for 500 g (1 lb)

Burger
2,500 l (660 gal) water for
1 burger (150g / 5oz beef)

Cheese
2,500 l (660 gal) water
for 500g (1 lb)

Millet
2,500 l (660 gal) water
for 500g (1 lb)

Beef
4,650 l (1,230 gal) water
for 1 steak (300g / 10 oz)

B

as they often are in large-scale animal husbandry. However, progress is being made on this front. The use of antibiotics in broiler chicken has reduced in Britain dramatically since 2012. It now accounts for 22% of antibiotic use in meat production even though poultry makes up about 50% of the meat eaten. Due to public demand, and a new expectation in many circles that poultry be free of antibiotics, large producers are reducing their use in the USA, too. Perdue Farms, for example, has become 98 to 99% antibiotic free and other producers are following suit.

A   This map from 2010 shows that the use of antibiotics in livestock remains highly concentrated in industrialized countries, but is steadily becoming widespread globally.

B   These statistics show water use for different foodstuffs, according to waterfootprint.org. They illustrate how most animal products require far more water than the majority of plant-based foods.

Overall, a meat eater's diet uses 17 times more land, 14 times more water and 10 times more energy than that of a vegan. Part of this equation is that we use so much land to grow crops to feed the animals we eat. Of the 5 billion hectares of agricultural land on the planet, we use almost 70% to graze or grow feed for livestock. About 40% of the grains grown and a quarter of a million tons of soybeans go to feed livestock each year. The treatment of animals and its environmental impact has spurred several start-ups to grow cultured meat, or muscle grown in a lab from animal stem cells. In 2019, 115 grams (4 oz) of such meat costs about $600 to produce; but that's down from $300,000 in 2013. And created with no killing, no mistreatment, and a very different environmental footprint.

A

Overfished is a term used to describe when more fish are taken from a wild population than can be reproduced, thus decreasing the number of that type of fish over time.

By-catch is anything caught up in a fishing net that the fishermen cannot or do not intend to sell. It can include dolphins, turtles, sharks and other species of fish. By-catch is often killed in the process of being caught.

Aquaculture is the raising and harvesting of fish and seafood in a contained environment.

The environmental impact of eating animals does not stop on land. Declining fish populations around the world, destruction of environments by fishing methods and increased ocean pollution are all results of eating fish and seafood.

In 2016, almost 90% of fish stocks were fully fished or overfished, up from about 65% in 2000. By 2016, people were eating an average of 20 kg (44 lb) of fish a year, compared to only 10 kg (22 lb) in the 1960s. To fish on this scale, the industry has developed technologies that further harm the environment: hooks and nets that scrape the ocean floor and huge nets that catch things other than the intended types of fish, which results in by-catch.

Most aquaculture does not fare much better. While positive strides have been made, the practice tends to use more resources, often smaller fish, to produce the fish it grows, thus leading to a net loss of energy. Additional problems include antibiotic use and pollution from the feed used in open-water pens, as well as the escape of farmed fish into wild populations, which can spread disease or introduce new genetics. Some aquaculture, particularly of bivalves such as oysters, mussels and clams, is environmentally sustainable and can help clean waterways.

For strict vegans, even an environmentally helpful oyster bed is exploitative. For those driven by environmental concerns, however, the aquaculture of bivalves is a culinary and ecological boon.

A   Frozen tuna await auction at Tokyo's Tsukiji fish market. The popularity of sushi outside of Japan has driven up demand for tuna. Several bluefin and bigeye species are already considered endangered

B   Trawling – or fishing by dragging a net either through the ocean or along the ocean floor – is a particularly destructive fishing method because it indiscriminately picks up anything in its wake.

C   Purse seine fishing isolates an area and draws the targeted section together, pulling anything in it up and out of the water. It tends to result is less by-catch than trawling.

While altruism and sustainability may be the focus of some vegans, many others are today compelled by personal health. A vegan diet has been connected to a wide range of health benefits.

A

In general, vegans tend to eat more dietary fibre and take in more polyunsaturated fatty acids, folic acid, vitamins C and E, magnesium and even iron. A vegan diet also tends to be lower in calories, saturated fat and cholesterol. All of these elements have health implications. Vegans tend to have lower bad cholesterol, lower blood pressure, a reduced risk of heart disease and lower rates of type 2 diabetes. They even have a lesser risk of certain cancers.

Type 2 diabetes, formerly known as adult onset diabetes, means the body either does not produce enough insulin or cannot utilize the insulin it does produce, thus making it difficult for the body to use or process glucose in the blood. In turn, this raises blood sugar levels and leads to a range of symptoms, including fatigue, kidney problems, vision loss and circulation issues. Without proper care, it can lead to heart attack or stroke.

Cholesterol is a fat-like substance that is needed to build cells and make hormones as well as other bodily functions. Our bodies make all the cholesterol they require. Consequently, ingesting additional cholesterol can increase the amount in our bodies, particularly of LDL, or the 'bad' kind of cholesterol, in our blood. Too much cholesterol can block arteries or cause increased blood pressure or heart disease.

Saturated fat is any fat that turns solid at room temperature. It is found in meat, eggs, dairy and some fish and shellfish, as well as in coconut oil and palm oil.

Since vegans do not eat any animal products – and cholesterol comes solely from animal products – it is no surprise that they have a lower risk of developing diseases connected to high cholesterol.

In addition, vegans tend to eat less saturated fat than meat eaters. While some tropical oils, such as coconut oil and palm oil, contain saturated fat, most saturated fat is found in animal products. In the traditional Western pattern diet, with its focus on meat, people tend to take in far more saturated fat than is considered healthy. The average Briton, for example, eats 29% more saturated fat than is recommended, while the average American eats 18% more than recommended. Of course, there is the French paradox: French people consume far more animal fat than Americans – 108 grams (3¾ oz) compared to 72 grams (2½ oz)– and yet have much lower rates of heart disease. This contradiction has been explained in many ways, including theories about higher levels of red wine consumption, but overall there appears to be no real paradox: the French may consume more animal fat, but this is within an overall diet that is otherwise filled with fruits, vegetables and other whole ingredients.

Even the most healthy meat is going to have some cholesterol and saturated fat. The least nutritious will contain high levels, and, if processed, is likely to include high amounts of sodium and possibly additives. In 2015, the World Health Organization went so far as to categorize processed meat as 'carcinogenic' (cancer causing), along with asbestos and arsenic.

A   Although the connection between a diet heavy in red meat and potential health problems is no secret, the Heart Attack Grill in Las Vegas, Nevada, offers its customers large portions of food that is high in fat and cholesterol.

B   On *Man v. Food*, the host travels the USA eating regional foods and taking on 'big food' challenges, from eating super spicy food or 2-kg (4-lb) sandwiches to downing large pitchers of Bloody Marys.

B

Since our bodies use saturated fat to make cholesterol, eating a lot of saturated fat can lead to higher cholesterol levels. So, again, it is not surprising that vegans have fewer problems with high cholesterol.

Furthermore, better cholesterol numbers tend to be associated with lower blood pressure. If arteries become narrowed or blocked, the heart has to work harder to pump blood through them, thus raising blood pressure. This is why both high cholesterol and increased blood pressure are linked to an augmented risk of heart disease: the heart is working harder to do the same job and blockages can occur in the heart muscle itself. With high blood pressure also comes a greater risk of stroke and of developing dementia.

It is not that vegans cannot have high blood pressure or develop heart disease, but a vegan diet lowers the risk of such problems. In fact, an animal-free diet is sometimes prescribed as a way to bring down blood pressure or to recover from heart disease. Importantly, benefits are seen with a reduction of meat eating as well. It's not an all-or-nothing game.

A

A   Affordable vegan meal plans are easy to achieve and include lots of nutritious vegetables, whole grains and legumes.

B   Around the world, governments, NGOs and schools offer classes to teach people how to make healthy, plant-based meals with fresh ingredients. Here, patients who have hypertension and/or diabetes learn to make salad dressing at the Brockton Neighborhood Health Center, MA.

B

The relationship between veganism and a decreased risk of type 2 diabetes is equally straightforward. Diet and weight are significant factors contributing to the development of this condition. A diet rich in whole grains, legumes, nuts, seeds and produce (one that vegans tend to eat) and staying lean (as vegans tend to do) lower the risk of developing the disease.

There is also evidence that a vegan diet can help combat inflammatory diseases such as many auto-immune disorders, irritable bowel syndrome and allergies. Some people have success keeping chronic conditions such as arthritis in check by following a vegan diet.

A Mechanically separated chicken is made by passing the bones of a butchered chicken through a sieve under high pressure to 'recover' the last bits of meat. The process results in an unappetizing pink paste.

B Billy Bear Slicing Sausage is a highly processed meat product aimed at children. It is made from about one-third turkey, one-third pork and one-third a mix of pork fat, pork liver and pea and carrot fibre.

C This globally inspired vegan spread features tortillas, guacamole, olives, pepper salad, hummus, baguette and a grain salad.

Initial research suggests that vegans' high consumption of fruits and vegetables compared to meat eaters results in lower rates of prostate and colorectal cancer. A 2014 study at Oxford University found the overall cancer rate was 11% lower among vegetarians than meat-eaters and 19% lower in vegans. The reason – more produce, less meat, or something else – was not determined, but the lower rates were backed up by the findings of several other studies, and separate studies have found that a diet rich in plant-based foods decreases the risk of many types of cancer.

By not eating any animal products, vegans avoid not only the health risks associated with higher saturated fat intake, but also a host of other possible diseases, including BSE and listeria. Greater regulation over the use of mechanically recovered meat, which is produced by grinding and sieving carcasses to separate the last bit of meat from the bones of a slaughtered animal, has decreased the health risks associated with this meat paste, but it has not eliminated them. Yet mechanically recovered meat is part of our food system, 'ick' factor and all.

Many people take up a vegan diet in the hope of losing weight.

It tends to work, even when calorie restriction is not the goal. On the whole, vegans are slimmer than meat eaters, and also record a slighter lower average BMI than lacto-ovo-vegetarians. While there is nothing about veganism that is inherently slimming – a person can overload on calories and eat a diet of fried potatoes and sweets and still be vegan – for many people who try it, cutting calorie-dense animal products out of their diet leads to weight loss or an easier time maintaining a desired weight.

BSE (bovine spongiform encephalopathy) is commonly known as 'mad cow disease'. People contract it from eating meat, particularly matter from the brain or spinal cord, of infected cows.

Listeria is a bacterium found in delicatessen meats and fresh raw-milk cheeses. It can lead to miscarriage in pregnant women and foodborne illnesses in others.

BMI (body mass index), or Quetelet index, is a person's weight in kilograms divided by their height in metres. The resulting number helps health professionals screen for weight categories that are associated with health problems. A person's BMI, however, is not in and of itself diagnostic.

c

A

Along with weight loss, many vegans report clear skin, stronger nails and glossier hair. Some also note higher energy levels and better sleep patterns while eating vegan. If vanity is the subject, a 2006 study published in *Chemical Senses* found that women preferred the smell of men who followed a vegan diet.

Today's vegan advocates tend to emphasize their diet as a nutritious and delicious option, not just an ethical one. As a result, more and more cookbooks, apps, courses and online videos are available for those looking to give up animal products.

For people who love animals and are seeking a more compassionate existence, the personal benefits of being vegan are far greater than a flat stomach and decreased health risks. For them, avoiding animal products is a benefit unto itself. They find it morally, philosophically and even spiritually fulfilling to live in what they see as a more compassionate way.

Vegans tend to know far more about what is in their food and how it was made. That curiosity applies to other lifestyle products and culminates in an awareness whose political and economic impact is beginning to be felt.

3. The Challenges of Veganism

A

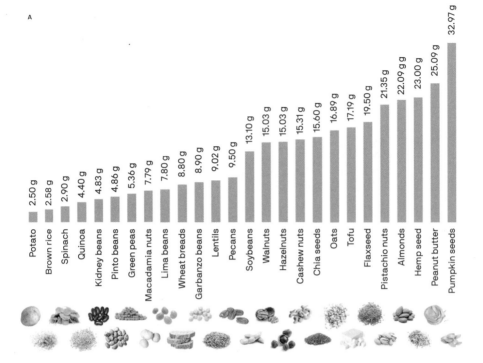

Potato 2.50 g
Brown rice 2.58 g
Spinach 2.90 g
Quinoa 4.40 g
Kidney beans 4.83 g
Pinto beans 4.86 g
Green peas 5.36 g
Macadamia nuts 7.79 g
Lima beans 7.80 g
Wheat breads 8.80 g
Garbanzo beans 8.90 g
Lentils 9.02 g
Pecans 9.50 g
Soybeans 13.10 g
Walnuts 15.03 g
Hazelnuts 15.03 g
Cashew nuts 15.31 g
Chia seeds 15.60 g
Oats 16.89 g
Tofu 17.19 g
Flaxseed 19.50 g
Pistachio nuts 21.35 g
Almonds 22.09 g g
Hemp seed 23.00 g
Peanut butter 25.09 g
Pumpkin seeds 32.97 g

There are many positive reasons to turn
to veganism, but the challenges cluster
around individual concerns, such as getting
adequate nutrition and the difficulties of
sticking to a restrictive diet.

The first subject that comes up is protein. Can vegans eat enough protein without protein-rich animal products? How can they do this? What happens when they inevitably do not get adequate protein? Protein, protein, protein!

Animal products do have high levels of protein – beef and other meats contain 25 to 30 grams (approx 1 oz) of protein per 100 grams (3½ oz), cheddar has 25 grams (1 oz) and salmon 20 grams (¾ oz)– so the concern makes sense. Yet, the idea that animal products are the only good or sufficient source of protein is unfounded.

Indeed, eating less protein than we do now would be fine. The recommended daily amount is 0.75 grams (¹⁄₃₂ oz) of protein per kilogram (2¼ lb) of body weight, which averages out to be 45 grams (1½ oz) for sedentary women and 55 grams (2 oz) for sedentary men. Active people require more protein, but not much more. However, the average French person, like the average American, eats 113 grams (4 oz) of protein a day: more than twice as much as needed. The rest of Europe hovers above 100 grams (3½ oz), while Israel tops out at 126 grams (4½ oz). Japan, by contrast, averages 92 grams (3¼ oz) of protein per person per day, which is still significantly more than our bodies need.

Protein, along with fat and carbohydrate, is one of the macronutrients that make up human food. The body uses protein to build and repair muscles, bones, skin and blood, as well as to create enzymes and hormones.

A   It is perfectly possible for humans to get all the protein they need from plant-based foods. This chart shows the number of grams of protein found per 100 g (3½ oz) of 26 common vegan foods.

B   On average, animal-based foods contain significantly more protein per 100 g (3½ oz) than plant-based foods.

C   Pulses and beans, aka legumes, are an important source of protein within a plant-based diet. They include all types of beans, lentils, peanuts and split peas.

B

C

The reason many people associate animal products with protein is not restricted to the high levels; it is how nutrition is taught. Protein examples, or the place on the plate for protein, are too frequently represented by animal products only. This is partly a reflection of tradition in Western diets, and partly due to the historical power of the meat, egg and dairy industries to shape nutritional information.

What surprises many people is just how much protein can be found in plenty of plant foods. Soy products such as tofu, tempeh and edamame have between 10% and 19% of protein. Chickpeas and other beans contain around 15% protein, while lentils and other pulses tend to include about 9%. Seitan packs a punch at a meaty 25%. Numerous other plant-based foods have decent amounts of protein. Oatmeal has 17% and green peas 8%. All grains and vegetables contain some protein. Artichokes include 4%, broccoli and rice each around 3%, lettuce just over 1% and carrots just under 1%. Another good plant source for a big hit of protein is nutritional yeast, which contains 60 grams of protein per 100 grams (2 oz per 3½ oz), although that would be a lot of nutritional yeast to eat!

A

GROUP ONE

GROUP SEVEN

GROUP TWO

GREEN AND YELLOW VEGETABLES...
some raw—some cooked, frozen or canned

BUTTER AND FORTIFIED MARGARINE
(with added Vitamin A)

ORANGES, TOMATOES, GRAPEFRUIT...
or raw cabbage or salad greens

U.S. NEEDS US STRONG
★ EAT THE BASIC 7 EVERY DAY ★

GROUP SIX

GROUP THREE

BREAD, FLOUR, AND CEREALS...
Natural whole grain— or enriched or restored

POTATOES AND OTHER VEGETABLES AND FRUITS...
raw, dried, cooked, frozen or canned

MEAT, POULTRY, FISH, OR EGGS...
or dried beans, peas, nuts, or peanut butter

MILK AND MILK PRODUCTS...
fluid, evaporated, dried milk, or cheese

GROUP FIVE

GROUP FOUR

A This wheel chart from 1943 shows the seven different types of food that need to be combined in a 'balanced diet'. Throughout the 20th century, a balanced diet was assumed to contain a fair amount of animal products.

B Vegan chicken and burgers, such as these by Temple of Seitan, are usually made from soy products, with added flavour from vegetables, legumes, nuts, seeds, spices and herbs.

Tempeh is a fermented soy product that, because of the fermentation, also contains trace amounts of vitamin B12, magnesium and phosphorus.

Edamame are young soybeans, usually steamed or boiled in their pods. They are often eaten as a snack, but can be used in salads, stir frys and other dishes.

Nutritional yeast is a deactivated strain of *Saccharomyces cerevisiae* yeast. It packs 14 grams (½ oz) of protein , plus 7 grams (¼ oz) of fibre, for every 28-gram (1-oz) serving. It has a deeply savoury, cheesy flavour, making it a go-to option for vegans looking to add umami to their pasta, potatoes or even popcorn. It is sold in delicate flakes or a yellow powder.

A **'complete protein'** is a protein made up of all of the essential amino acids we need: tryptophan, threonine, isoleucine, leucine, lysine, methionine+cysteine, phenylalanine+tyrosine, valine and histidine. They are 'essential' because the body cannot make them; we must ingest them.

B

The good news for vegans is that all that protein adds up.

Contrary to popular belief, the notion of needing 'complete protein' – that only meat, fish and eggs provide it, and that other sources need to be combined to make it – is not true.

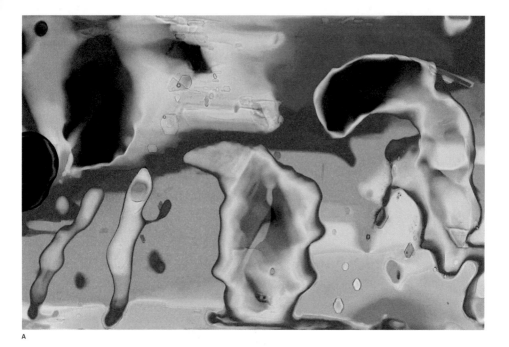

A

The idea of complete protein was introduced in 1909 by Karl Heinrich Ritthausen (1826–1912), a German biochemist. He identified glutamic acid and aspartic acid, which helped open up the idea that there are different kinds of plant protein. Meat, fish and eggs all contain all nine essential amino acids. Other foods only provide some of them. The belief that plant proteins are 'incomplete' because they do not have all nine was backed up by what is now seen as an inadequate study carried out at Yale University in 1914. From that, a theory developed that foods that contain some of the essential amino acids need to be eaten in combination, so that the diner gets all nine in one meal.

This theory was brought to widespread public attention in 1954 with the publication of Adelle Davis's book *Let's Eat Right to Keep Fit*, which stresses the importance of getting enough complete protein. It was further entrenched in popular thinking by Frances Moore Lappé's *Diet for a Small Planet* (1971), which explains at length the need to eat plant foods in the correct combinations to obtain complete proteins each day.

None of this is correct. Certainly, there are nine essential amino acids, but there is no reason to eat them all at once or on the same day or even in the same week. Lappé apologized in the 1981 revision of her book for having overly complicated a plant-based diet in her original publication.

Our bodies know that they are not always going to get all nine essential amino acids at once and plan accordingly. We are anatomically designed to push protein that is already in our bodies back into our digestive tract, needed or not, to be mixed and matched with whatever we are eating that day.

So, the challenge of getting enough protein from a vegan diet is only a problem if someone wilfully ignores basic information and a bevy of delicious foods.

A   Serine amino acid, seen here in a light micrograph, is considered a non-essential amino acid, not because our bodies do not need it, but because we can synthesize it under normal conditions.

B   It is important to use the right type of tofu in each recipe. Silken tofu, for example, has a silky-smooth texture and is ideal in creamy desserts. Firm and extra firm tofu have the lowest moisture content and work well in pan-fried and baked recipes.

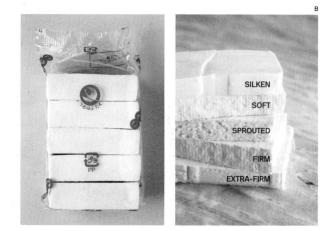

SILKEN

SOFT

SPROUTED

FIRM

EXTRA-FIRM

Protein deficiency may be a red herring when it comes to being vegan, but the possible lack of various vitamins, minerals and other micronutrients in plant-based foods deserves more serious attention.

Vegan diets are naturally lower in micronutrients that concentrate in animal products, such as vitamin B12, omega-3 fatty acids (also known as long-chain n-3 fatty acids), calcium, zinc and vitamin D. Iron can be a challenge, too, depending on an individual's taste for dark leafy greens.

The only micronutrient that is truly difficult to get from plant-based foods, unless you eat a large quantity of tempeh, is vitamin B12. However, this problem can be solved by taking supplements, and many common vegan foods, such as soy products and nut milks, are fortified with B12.

A

A   Rexford Hitchcock of Great Earth vitamin store in San Francisco demonstrates how to take a gel form of B12 through the nose. B12 is notoriously more difficult to obtain in a plant-based diet than other vitamins, but there are many ways to supplement a vegan diet.

B   Concerns about being able to obtain enough protein from a plant-based diet are undercut by vegan professional body-builders like Patrik Baboumian.

Micronutrients are nutrients that the body needs in small amounts, such as vitamins and minerals.

Vitamin B12 is essential for the nervous system and blood cells. A lack of vitamin B12 can cause fatigue and depression-like symptoms. While it is only available through animal food sources and tempeh, vegan supplements derive vitamin B12 from bacteria.

Fatty acids are important to heart health, having been proven to help regulate triglycerides or blood fat levels. They have also been shown to affect depression and brain development.

Calcium is an essential mineral. While most people associate it with bone and dental health, it also helps blood to clot, muscles to contract and hearts to beat.

Zinc is one of the nutrients that affect the body's ability to process and use protein effectively. It also helps immune systems to fight bacteria and viruses.

Vitamin D has a role in several bodily functions, but most importantly it allows the body to absorb calcium. Thus, it is critical for bone growth and maintenance. Too little vitamin D in children can lead to rickets or soft bones, and too little in adults can cause fragile bones.

Iron is so critical to the body that a lack of it has a name: anaemia. A lack of iron leads to fatigue, since the body uses it to make haemoglobin, which carries oxygen from the lungs through the bloodstream to the rest of the body.

Dark leafy greens such as kale, collard green, beet greens and turnip greens are nutritionally impressive. Exact amounts vary, but dark leafy greens tend to be loaded in iron and calcium, and even omega-3 fatty acids. They are also full of dietary fibre, and vitamins C, E and K.

B

Most of the other micronutrients found in heavy concentration in animal products can also be found in plant-based foods. Omega-3 fatty acids, for example, are widely associated with salmon and cod liver oil. However, they are present in plant sources such as chia seeds, hemp seeds, flax seeds, canola oil, walnuts and leafy greens, which means omega-3 fatty acids can easily be included in a healthy vegan diet. Similarly, calcium is mainly associated with dairy products. Although milk contains a lot of calcium, there are plenty of plant sources for calcium, most notably dark leafy greens such as kale, turnip greens and seaweed.

Choline is a lesser-known micronutrient, necessary to the proper functioning of the metabolism.

Choline is a trace mineral present in eggs and organ meat, as well as in cruciferous vegetables such as broccoli, cauliflower, cabbage and sprouts. Consequently, only vegans who dislike these types of vegetables are in danger of missing out. Zinc is found in large amounts in meat, poultry and seafood, especially oysters, but it is also in beans and legumes, nuts and seeds, oatmeal and nutritional yeast.

Vitamin D is more difficult than other micronutrients to get from plant sources. It is seen as a dairy nutrient, but this is only because milk is almost always fortified with it. Vegan foods such as tofu, soy milk and almond milk are also fortified with vitamin D. In addition, we can find it in mushrooms and good old-fashioned sunshine. Iron is commonly associated with meat. Luckily for vegans, the amounts needed are easily met through lentils, dark leafy greens and many grains, nuts and seeds.

Getting proper micronutrient nutrition is a definite challenge for many people who switch to veganism, but it is entirely possible.

A

On a personal yet less technical or nutritional level, switching to a vegan diet can be challenging for a range of reasons. If nothing else, it can be difficult because it eliminates entire food groups that are beloved and common in many cultures. Men can find it particularly challenging because of cultural notions of the 'manly' nature of a meat-and-potatoes diet, and a lifetime of habits formed around that association. Since on average men need more protein than women, a switch to a vegan diet can seem like more of a hurdle for men.

Vegans have to seek out more variety from fewer food types or risk having a limited diet.

They need to make an effort to keep their diet as varied as possible, mixing up types of grains, legumes and produce to embrace nutritional and culinary variety: in other words, they have to apply forethought and planning to their meals.

A   The various B vitamins, iron and calcium found in dark leafy greens, such as the kale being harvested here, are important in a vegan diet. Plus, a large part of the small amount of fat that kale has is alpha-linolenic acid, which is an omega-3 fatty acid.
B   Plant-based 'milk' products made from soy, almonds, hemp or oatmeal are extremely popular with vegans and widely available. Most of the milks are enriched with vitamins and minerals, and many are sweetened or flavoured.

B

A

A   The myriad of food labels working to make ethical and environmentally sound food choices easier can be confusing. Vegans should look for labels that are certified or independently verified.

B   People may be surprised that most gummy sweets are not vegan, but gelatin is made from animal collagen. Vegan versions exist, made using agar or carrageenan, both of which derive from seaweed.

While vegan labels on food are making it easier to shop, and there is an increasing number of vegan options in grocery stores all the time, there is still a great deal to take on board and many foods or food production techniques that strict vegans will want to avoid.

As of writing, vegan labels are not regulated by any countrywide definitions in Britain or the EU, although such standards are in the pipeline. Similarly, there are no legal definitions of either 'vegetarian' or 'vegan' for food labels in the USA. Around the world, the labels 'vegetarian' or 'vegan' on food are more of a marketing tool than a regulatory one: manufacturers are responsible for their own definitions and held to account by consumers, not third-party verification. Even in India, where since 2011 manufacturers must mark packaged food with a green dot for vegetarian and a brown dot for non-vegetarian, the labels are not independently verified.

For dedicated vegans, there are a lot of commonly used ingredients beyond the obvious – meat, fish, eggs, milk – that need to be avoided, including any foods that contain elements derived from animal products, such as gelatin and whey, both of which are common ingredients in prepared and processed foods. Gelatin is used in a wide range of confectionery, including gummy sweets and marshmallows, as well as in less obvious places such as in some roasted peanuts (it helps the salt or other seasonings adhere to the nuts). Whey, once a waste product that was sometimes fed to animals or sprayed onto fields as a fertilizer, is now found in many foods, such as baked goods, beverages and sweets, as well as in a wide array of dairy products. Because it is high in protein, it is also commonly used to make protein powder as a nutritional supplement.

Even foods that are marked 'dairy-free' or 'lactose-free' are not necessarily vegan: the labels are aimed at people with that particular dietary restriction. Some non-vegan ingredients have names that obscure their sources, such as albumin, a protein from egg white, or casein, a protein from milk.

Gelatin is made from animal bones, collagen and connective tissue. It is used as a thickener and stabilizer.

Whey is the liquid that is left after milk is curdled and the curds are removed to make cheese.

B

The question of trace amounts of ingredients begs the question of who can call themselves a vegan? It is shocking to many, but wine and beer, while made from plants, are not necessarily vegan. So, if you do not eat meat, fish, eggs or dairy but do not worry too much about how your wine gets clarified can you still claim to be vegan?

Most wines are clarified using a process called 'fining', which employs various animal products to get the naturally occurring protein in wine to bind with the protein in the fining agent. Both proteins are then removed from the wine, resulting in a clear rather than hazy or cloudy liquid.

A A vintner at Château Lynch-Bages, France, demonstrates the truly old-school way of fining wine with egg whites. Most modern producers buy the protein albumin, which attaches to tannins and impurities, already separated out from the actual egg.

B Some vegan beer makers do more than skip the animals products to clarify or fine their beer. Yulli's Brews opened a plant-based taproom and restaurant in Sydney, Australia, in 2018, and Alternation Brewing Co. now offer a milk stout made with almond milk. The beer comes in several flavour variants, such as the OREO version seen here.

A

B

White, rosé and sparkling wines typically add isinglass, a fish protein, for fining, whereas red wine usually uses albumin or casein. In all cases, the animal products are removed from the wine before bottling, but their use renders the wine not vegan. Fruit juices are sometimes similarly clarified. Vegan wines are either left to self-clarify or clarified using activated charcoal or bentonite, a type of clay made from weathered volcanic ash.

Most beers contain only water, barley malt, hops and yeast and so are vegan. However, some brewers adopt the same fining process as winemakers to create a clear, non-cloudy beer. In beer making, fining may utilise plant products, such as Irish moss, or it may use animal products, including isinglass or gelatin. These items do not appear in the list of ingredients because they are not in the final product.

A

Another problematic food is sugar. In the USA, refined cane sugar is sometimes whitened with bone char. Consequently, vegans need to use unrefined sugar or brands that do not include bone char; surprisingly, brown sugar is not necessarily vegan because it is made by adding molasses back into refined white sugar.

A   Many soy products, such as tofu seen drying here, are traditional foods in Asian cuisines. Vegans looking for minimally processed protein sources can find tofu and other soy products made in small batches by hand.

B   Other vegan protein products are more industrial, such as these meat-free Quorn products made in Stokesley, UK. Ingredient labels help decipher if a product is made from whole foods, such as mushrooms, soy and nuts, or more highly processed elements.

Vegans will also want to watch out for L-cysteine, an amino acid derived from human hair or poultry feathers that shows up as a softening agent in breads, and castoreum, an anal secretion from beavers that can be used as an artificial vanilla scent and flavour. The latter is now mainly used in fragrances rather than foodstuffs, but can be legally included as a 'natural flavour'. When used as supplements in foods, omega-3 fatty acids are often derived from fish, so 'heart healthy' orange juice may include sardines, even if the fish are not listed in the ingredients.

This may all seem like needless nit-picking, but strict vegans do not eat anything that has been processed with animal products, even if the final product is animal-free. When we talk about whether we should all be vegan, we need a full picture of what that could (or should, according to some) mean.

While some vegan advocates are researching labels and calling manu-facturers, other food activists are troubled by specifically vegan products. A number of these, including meat substitutes, are highly processed. Although this is acceptable to many vegans, particularly those who choose not to eat animal products for ethical reasons, the issue becomes murkier for those interested in sustainability and quality food. Almost any vegan meat substitute is more sustainable than, say, industrial feedlot beef, but it may not be more sustainable than a pasture-raised chicken.

A

Then there are the genetically modified organisms (GMOs). While everyone should have questions about the process of inserting the genes of one species – be it plant, bacteria, virus, animal or human – into the genes of another, vegans have extra reasons to be concerned. This is exemplified by the Flavr Savr, also known as the fish tomato. Engineered to have a longer shelf life and to withstand chilling using GMO technology, it contained an anti-freeze gene from an Arctic fish. The tomato never made it to market. The rats on which one line of the tomatoes were tested died at a higher rate than other rats, so the company that developed Flavr Savr voluntarily pulled it from consideration. But its existence begs the question: Is a tomato containing a fish gene vegan?

In the EU, GMOs need to be labelled as such, but in the USA, no such rules apply. Although foods that are marked 'organic' cannot contain GMOs, this is the only way that a consumer would know whether a product contained a GMO.

B

The confusion around labels and identifying vegan foods can create difficulties when eating out.

A/B Beekeepers demonstrating at Monsanto headquarters in France and environmentalists protesting GMO corn imports to South Korea both advocate for the precautionary principle: until we know more and can guarantee they do no harm, stop the widespread use of GMOs. Other activists work to ensure that products containing GMOs are properly labelled – something that is mandated in the EU but not in the USA.

There has been a huge growth in the availability of vegan dishes in cafés and restaurants, and in many cities there are outlets that serve only vegan food. However, vegans still often face limited choices. Chicken broth lurks in soups, fish sauce pops up in Vietnamese and Thai food, and whey hides in bread.

Restricted options are almost certain at social gatherings, too. Of course, the extent to which being vegan impacts anyone's social life depends on their social circle, but the limitation, inconvenience and awkwardness of being vegan is a challenge for many. Humans have enjoyed centuries – nay, millennia – of bonding over shared meals. Not to partake, to stand apart in what one eats is, in many cultures, not to belong.

So, the potential marginalizing effects of a vegan diet should not be downplayed, nor should the difficulty of trying to stick to the diet in the face of societal and social adversity. Social pressure is real, and the conditioning of our food preferences by experience, advertising and educators is immense.

A vegan diet also necessitates a change in cooking habits. It can be difficult to locate a variety of prepared vegan foods, so many vegans find themselves cooking from scratch, especially if they want to avoid processed foods. For people with a love of and curiosity about food, this can mean exploring exciting new cuisines, but for others more time in the kitchen is a chore. Supermarkets are responding to the increasing number of people who are exploring a vegan lifestyle and are stocking their shelves accordingly.

A

B

A These colourful pre-prepared meals feature vegan food as it is most commonly presented, composed of fruits, vegetables and grains.

B By contrast, @uglyvegan on Instagram challenges society's restrictive view of vegan food by showing that there is much more on offer than raw veg and seeds, and by abandoning both the didactic tone and focus on health that is often associated with veganism.

One discomforting personal issue for a vegan is the impact of extra dietary fibre on the body's digestive system. People who are not used to it may experience an uncomfortable amount of gas and bloating at first. However, once the body adjusts to digesting more fibre, the symptoms usually subside.

Yet, the challenges of veganism extend beyond individual inconvenience and nutrition.

Another practical consideration is fertilizer. Most farmers agree that the most effective ones come from manure. However, a strict vegan, who opposes the exploitation of animals by humans, would be against using manure, thus frustrating the production of vegan foodstuffs. If humans are not raising livestock, access to large amounts of manure will end.

Dietary fibre is a carbohydrate that humans cannot digest. It is found in large amounts in whole grains, produce and legumes.

Manure can be composted, or allowed to decompose, often with additional plant material before being sold as fertilizer.

A

B

Two solutions exist.

The first calls for the use of synthetic fertilizers. These are amazingly effective at helping plants grow, but they do next to nothing for the health of the soil. Repeated applications can even lead to the build-up of toxic compounds such as arsenic. This is why synthetic fertilizers are not allowed in organic farming. In short, this 'solution' would undo a fair amount of the environmental benefit of veganism. Since interest in veganism has developed hand in glove with organic farming since the 1970s, balancing the need for effective organic fertilizers and zero animal husbandry would be difficult.

Synthetic fertilizers, also known as chemical fertilizers, are made of inorganic rather than organic compounds. They are most often derived from petroleum products. The process for making synthetic fertilizers was developed in the early 20th century. Their use after World War II led to the Green Revolution in the 1950s and 1960s. Along with the development of high-yield crops, synthetic fertilizers changed the way we grow food.

Green manure is the practice of growing a crop and tilling it back into the field to return nutrients to the soil and improve soil health. It is usually grown on a field after harvest or in the spring before planting.

Compost is organic matter, such as food waste and plant material, that is allowed to decompose. It becomes what gardeners and organic farmers call 'black gold' for its ability to add nutrients back into the soil.

Bees and other insects pollinate at least 30% of the fruits, vegetables and nuts that humans grow as crops (and up to 90% of wild plants). Vegan activists argue that letting natural bee populations grow would render beekeeping unnecessary. Many agricultural experts believe that plan to be unrealistic.

The second solution is a combination of green manure and compost. When combined, green manure and compost not only maintain soil health but also improve it, providing a net environmental benefit along with fertile fields. Growing green manure has been found to reduce the loss of nitrogen, a key element for most crops, by 97% compared to fields that are left bare after harvest. The main issue with green manure is that it requires both time and planning. It also lacks the impact of animal manure and cannot build up poor or overworked soils as quickly or effectively.

Relatedly, the widespread adoption of veganism raises the question of how to address pest control in farming. Pesticides kill animals, obviously. Although natural pest control is possible, it sometimes involves indirectly killing the pests, as well as exploiting other animals. Hardcore vegans are against keeping bees even for the pollination of crops, so using ladybugs and beneficial beetles for pest control is unacceptable, too.

A   Giant heaps of cow manure from a dairy farm dominate a cornfield in Heilongjiang province, China. The dairy produces more manure than can be effectively used on nearby farmland, so the waste soon piles up, emitting a noxious smell.

B   Rainfall washes fertilizers and other potential pollutants off farmland in Iowa and into the watershed. The main danger is the nitrates, which create dead zones in lakes and bays, and at high levels can contaminate water supplies.

C/D   Algae blooms, like the ones on Lake St Clair between Michigan and Ontario (top) and Taihu Lake in Wuxi, China (bottom), are occurring more and more frequently due to fertilizer run-off. The resultant excess nitrogen in the water encourages the rapid growth of algae and green plants. The blooms do not simply spoil the landscape; when extensive enough, they choke out other life in the water, including fish.

C

D

A   Community-supported agriculture, as seen at Huguenot Street Farm, is a model whereby customers buy a 'share' in a farm's harvest. Usually, they opt in at the start of the season and then receive a share of the harvest. The farm has money up-front and guaranteed sales; customers get farm-fresh produce all season long.

B   In poverty-stricken countries, children, like this young girl seated at a bus station in Korhogo, Ivory Coast, are in particular danger of being trafficked. Some are tricked into compliance and others are kidnapped to be used as servants or slave labour, particularly on cacao plantations.

Luckily, this extreme no-manure, no-pest control future is unlikely to occur. Switching to a plant-centric rather than a fully vegan diet is more realistic for many people, and that shift, with less meat produced and produced under better conditions, would turn our current state of an over-abundance of animal waste into one where it could all be used as fertilizer.

The issue of pest control highlights some ethical limitations of veganism. We can stop eating animals, and we can stop raising animals for our use in any way. We can even fertilize fields with vegan compost. But can we produce food without killing or harming any animals at all? No, we cannot. Simply tilling the soil and harvesting plants involves a level of carnage for insects, and sometimes birds and small mammals, too.

The unattainability of true veganism,
of living on the planet without ever
harming another living creature,
can be thrown up as an argument
against even trying a vegan lifestyle,
but that is a difficult position to defend.
The more interesting ethical question
is whether or not a vegan diet is
always and necessarily more
ethical than an omnivorous one.

It is possible to follow a strict vegan diet but eat
foods raised using slave labour, or that are grown
with harmful chemicals that are destructive to the
environment, or are grown in sacred ground. In this
way, a vegan diet could be more harmful than an
omnivorous one. This observation is not so much
a problem or downside of veganism as a tempering
of its espoused benefits. All advantages and all
challenges are part of a holistic system and are depen-
dent on how all food and lifestyle choices are made.

B

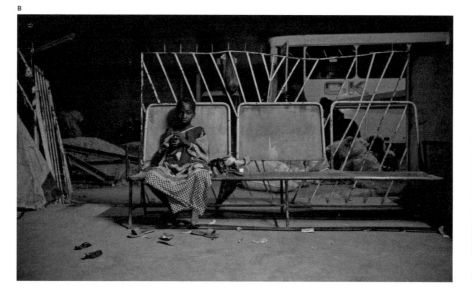

A

This brings us to the most nebulous but perhaps most difficult challenge of a vegan lifestyle: tradition. The issue is two-fold.

A   As the demand for quinoa has increased, not all of it is grown in the Andes anymore, nor is it winnowed, or sorted, in the traditional way seen here, using simply a plate and the ground.

B   Increasingly, quinoa is processed at large facilities, such as this one in Bolivia. A significant amount of quinoa is now being farmed in the USA and Canada to meet the growing demand for this nutritious, grain-like seed.

First, vegan preferences can disrupt traditional food systems. This can be caused by a shift in demand, efforts to hybridize or standardize seeds, or a co-option of production.

A fairly well-known example is quinoa, a seed that is cooked and used as a grain, native to the Andean Plateau in South America. It is a rare plant that contains all nine essential amino acids that humans need in their diet. When the demand for quinoa increased a decade ago, prices rose – tripling between 2006 and 2013 and becoming more expensive than chicken – and the people in its native region found themselves unable to afford a foodstuff that had sustained them for hundreds of years.

B

Similarly, in 2018, Mexico considered importing avocados, a fruit that originates in the country and has been a local staple for centuries, because its growing worldwide popularity had led to a national shortage.

Second, meat and other animal products play an essential role in many cultures and in traditional observations, rituals and practices. The switch to veganism could well be difficult to manage physically, psychologically and socially.

Traditions are powerful things. They bring people together and define identities.

What is Easter for Greek families without lamb? Can you make pot-au-feu without a chicken? Is an eggless, dripping-free Yorkshire pudding still a Yorkshire pudding? Is it a luau without kalua pork or salmon lomi lomi?

Traditions, especially beloved and delicious ones, are no small challenge to overcome.

4. A Vegan Planet

What would a planet of vegans look like? What kind of environmental, economic, public health and even social and cultural changes might happen as the result of a mass switch to animal-free diets and lifestyles?

It would be a radical U-turn for our planet to go vegan.

Between 1961 and 2010, the consumption of beef, sheep and goat meat more than doubled, according to the Food and Agricultural Organization of the United Nations. Pork and poultry consumption increased even more, growing by three and nine times, respectively. The most dramatic shift occurred in Japan, where a traditional diet of plant-based foods with a bit of seafood moved towards a far more meat-centric diet. The change is most telling in Tokyo, where general meat consumption increased by 160% between 1970 and 2005, and pork consumption grew by 90% in the same period.

A

The **Food and Agricultural Organization of the United Nations** is an agency focused on ensuring that people around the world have access to a sufficient amount of high-quality food.

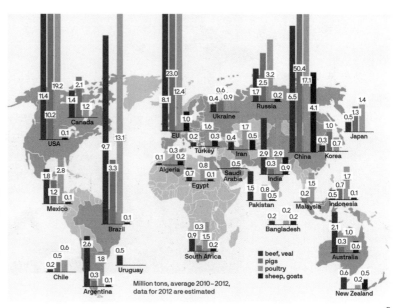

A A child digs into a meat treat at Disneyland, Tokyo, in this image from the *Common Sense* series (1998) by Martin Parr. It is an exploration of rampant consumerism around the world.

B This infographic shows worldwide meat production. The figures are independent of consumption, which would add a lot of arrows moving meat from South America to North America, for example.

USA 11.4 / 19.2 / 2.1 / 1.4 / 1.2
Canada 10.2 / 0.1
Mexico 1.8 / 2.8 / 1.2 / 0.1
Brazil 13.1 / 9.7 / 3.3 / 0.1
Chile 0.6 / 0.5 / 0.2
Argentina 2.6 / 1.8 / 0.3 / 0.1
Uruguay 0.5
EU 23.0 / 12.4 / 8.1 / 1.0
Algeria 0.3 / 0.1 / 0.2
Egypt 0.8 / 0.7 / 0.1
Turkey 1.6 / 0.2 / 0.3 / 0.4
Ukraine 0.6 / 0.4 / 0.9
Russia 3.2 / 2.5 / 1.7 / 0.2 / 6.5
Iran 1.7 / 0.5
Saudi Arabia 0.5
Iran 2.9 / 2.9 / 0.3
China 50.4 / 17.1 / 4.1 / 0.9
Korea 1.0 / 0.3 / 0.7
Japan 1.4 / 1.3 / 0.5
India 1.5 / 0.8 / 0.5
Pakistan 1.5 / 0.2 / 0.2
Malaysia 1.5 / 0.7 / 0.5 / 0.2
Indonesia 1.7 / 0.1
Bangladesh 0.3 / 0.9 / 1.5 / 0.2
South Africa 0.2
Australia 2.1 / 1.0 / 0.3 / 0.6
New Zealand 0.6 / 0.5 / 0.2

■ beef, veal
■ pigs
■ poultry
■ sheep, goats

Million tons, average 2010–2012, data for 2012 are estimated

B

Under current practices and demands, the global requirement for beef alone is projected to increase by 95% between 2015 and 2050. Demand for other kinds of meat has also been steadily growing in developing countries. In industrial countries, the average person eats 80 kilograms (176 lb) of meat each year. People in developing countries currently average just 32 kilograms (70.5 lb). There is every reason to think that as these economies grow, the demand for meat will increase, too.

A move towards widespread veganism would not only undo the effects of the consumption of animal products today, but also affect the future exponentially by cutting off the projected increase.

Some critics use the sheer number of animals already in existence to poke fun at those who would stop the raising of livestock, citing the fanciful issue of herds of cows suddenly let wild. While it is amusing to imagine chickens pecking in city parks and pigs cavorting in public fountains, any reasonable person would assume that animal farms would be phased out rather than closed overnight.

A

In fact, millions of animals would never be bred and raised; intensive animal husbandry operations and feedlots would close. Animal welfare issues in the agricultural space would become moot because there would not be any animals there.

Smaller, integrated farms that use the virtuous cycle to fertilize fields by pasturing animals on them for part of the year would need to move to methods that use only compost and green manure. Since this cycle is a fundamental practice on many organic farms, it is easy to imagine that some farms – especially those still in the process of rebuilding the health of the soil or where soil is naturally less robust – might need to turn to synthetic fertilizers to have an economically viable yield.

Regenerative agriculture projects that depend on domesticated animals to revitalize over-farmed land would be forced to stop under a truly vegan system. Efforts that rely on grazing animals to re-establish ecosystems, such as those that depend on the soil aeration, grass control and natural fertilizer provided by large grazing ruminants – bison in the western USA, for example – could conceivably release the animals to wild or federal grazing lands. However, without the oversight of moving the herds, the targeted regeneration would end.

B

Projects that harness the power of poultry – hunting and pecking while scratching the soil – to revive overused land would close.

Raising animals for food is inherently inefficient in terms of calories in and calories out.

Animals use as much as 90% of the food they eat to breathe, walk and reproduce; only about 10% is turned into muscle that becomes meat for humans to eat. Yet, animals, particularly ruminants such as cows and sheep, can eat things that humans cannot – large amounts of grass, for example. They can also make use of land that is not otherwise suited to raising food. Sheep may prefer lush green meadows, but they are capable of grazing on otherwise arid and thus unproductive land and have long provided an important food source in such areas. They have also been used as a form of weed control and have been shown to be as effective as herbicides on winter or fallow fields.

Regenerative agriculture is a set of varied farming practices that aim to enrich soil, improve watersheds and increase biodiversity.

Ecosystem refers to a biological community and how the members interact within a specific environment.

A   Farm animal sanctuaries, such as this one in the Catskills, New York, care for and protect animals that were once livestock.
B   These chickens have been rehomed. Some of them have very few feathers so their owner made hand-knitted sweaters to keep them warm.

A

Land used to graze sheep would likely return to nature, not food production. How people who depend on the calories and protein the sheep provide would fare is very much up for debate. In a vegan world, economies that rely on wool would require revamping. New Zealand's primary exports, for example, are beef, dairy, lamb and fish, as well as a smaller amount of machinery. The country would need an economic revolution.

The possibilities of regenerative agriculture and the ability of some animals to make use of otherwise unproductive land are good reasons to think about the role that reducing meat consumption, rather than rejecting it fully, could have.

Along with livestock, a global vegan diet would exclude wild game. Opinions vary on what would happen to wild animal populations that are currently controlled through regulated hunting. Would populations

Wild game includes boar, rabbit, deer, elk, pheasant, ducks and even moose, bear, reindeer or tiger, depending on where you live. In general, it is any animal hunted for food.

Bushmeat refers to any wild animal – mammal, reptile or bird – hunted for food in Africa.

Deforestation is the cutting down of forests and the elimination of forest land. It can be driven by logging, by the market for the wood of the trees themselves or by the desire for agricultural land.

explode without the check of hunting? Or would ecosystems find a new natural balance? Most likely, first the former and then the latter would happen.

A vegan planet would be beneficial for endangered species that are hunted or poached for their meat, such as elephants and rhinoceros. However, it could pose a problem to some human populations, such as the inhabitants of Central African countries for whom bushmeat – not factory-farmed animals – makes up 70% of the protein they consume.

Demand for bushmeat goes hand in hand with deforestation. As roads are built to facilitate logging, mining and other industries, they provide access for other users, thus increasing the likelihood of hunting and poaching. As wild animals and people are brought into closer contact, it rarely bodes well for the animals. The lion population in Africa, for example, has decreased 43% in just 20 years as agriculture has expanded onto their habitat. The decrease in their natural prey leads them to attack livestock, so farmers hunt them to protect their holdings.

B

A Technology gives humans a significant advantage when hunting, as shown by these stealthcam photographs that capture wild animals – deer and wolves – being monitored by bow-hunters.
B Bushmeat is sold at a public market in Bimbo, Central African Republic. Here, bushmeat is more than an important source of protein; it is also a key element of the informal economy and a conveyor of social status.

A

Deforestation also occurs to create new agriculture and grazing land, particularly in South America, where the worldwide demand for beef has made the clearing of rainforests to raise cattle profitable. By removing trees that transform carbon into oxygen, deforestation is contributing to global warming. The fewer trees, the more CO_2 stays in the atmosphere.

A The growing need for soy – driven more by the demand for animal feed than by humans' consumption of tofu – has led to vast tracks of farmland in South America being turned over to soy monoculture.

B Cattle walk a path along what was once Amazon rainforest. Agricultural, grazing and mining demands have led to an astonishing deforestation of the world's largest rainforest. More than 20% of it has already been destroyed, with more being cleared every year.

The need for land on which to grow soy plays a role in deforestation, too. Although a vegan planet would neces-sitate an increased demand for soy for human consumption,

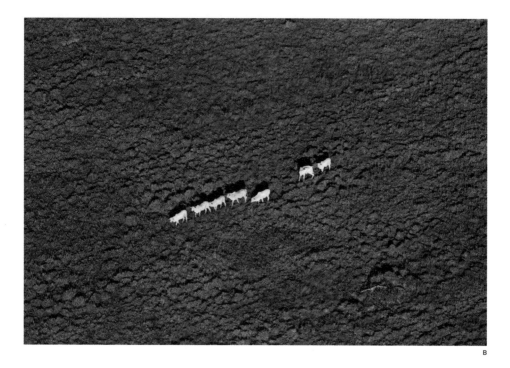

B

due to its high protein content, the soy currently grown for animal feed would likely more than fill that need: at present, approximately 85% of the global soy crop is processed into meal to feed animals. It is easy to speculate that no new deforestation would need to occur.

Another interesting consequence of a vegan planet is the potential positive impact that worldwide veganism might have on wild animal populations. According to the World Wildlife Fund and the Zoological Society of London, half of all wild animals were lost between 1970 and 2010. And the majority of those losses were in developing nations.

Methane gas is one of the most common organic compounds on Earth. It creates natural gas and it is in our bodily gas emissions. It makes up about 10% of greenhouse gases and has even more intense heat-trapping properties than the better-known carbon dioxide.

Greenhouse gas is any gas in the Earth's atmosphere that absorbs infrared radiation, thus trapping heat in the atmosphere and raising global temperatures. The main greenhouse gases are water vapour, carbon dioxide, methane, nitrous oxide and ozone.

Not needing additional grazing land to meet a seemingly endless appetite for beef would have a huge impact on the environment and the global economy, as would a halt to the hunting of wild animals for food.

Along with the phasing out of animal husbandry, antibiotics and other medications used for livestock would be removed from the system. Since approximately 80% of antibiotics produced world-wide are used on livestock, this would result in a dramatic decrease in the amount that finds its way into the ecosystem. It would also be a financial disaster for the pharmaceutical companies that make them. Moreover, environmental impacts from waste storage and run-off, as outlined in Chapter 2, would soon disappear.

A

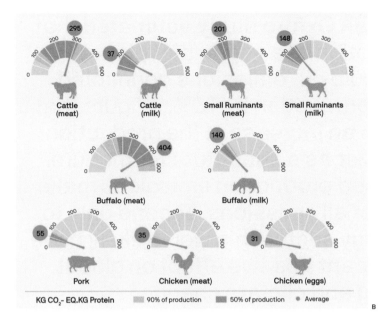

Cattle (meat) 295 · 37
Cattle (milk)
Small Ruminants (meat) 201
Small Ruminants (milk) 148
Buffalo (meat) 404
Buffalo (milk) 140
Pork 55
Chicken (meat) 35
Chicken (eggs) 31

KG CO$_2$- EQ.KG Protein   90% of production   50% of production   • Average

B

Additionally, global veganism would result in a decrease in methane gas and other pollutants. Livestock accounts for 66% of all agriculture-produced methane gas, even though it makes up only 37% of the total protein produced. Our use of farm animals also contributes a conservative estimate of 14% of all human greenhouse gas emissions. This figure is roughly equivalent to the amount of exhaust from every car, train, ship and airplane in the world.

A   Cows at Ellinbank Dairy Research Institute in Victoria, Australia, wear backpacks that measure their methane output as part of efforts to work out ways to reduce it.

B   This diagram shows the average CO$_2$ emissions of different animals per protein they produce. Thus buffalo meat has the highest emission intensity and chicken eggs the lowest. Intensity varies between producers however, due to different conditions and practices.

All mammals naturally produce methane gas, with every burp and every fart. Cattle are particularly flatulent, especially when they are fed a diet of grain (which is difficult for their bodies to process) instead of grass (which they have evolved to digest). They are larger than other livestock and are fed a diet that is unlike any they would naturally pursue, more so than any other livestock. The combination means that cattle produce three to four times more greenhouse gas emissions than any other animal we raise.

In 2016, an Oxford study estimated that the adoption of a vegan diet planet-wide would cut emissions connected to food production by 70%, a figure that includes an increase in the production of fertilizer as a substitute for manure. Since food production emissions make up 13% of all emissions, second only to the energy sector, this would likely have a significant positive effect on global warming and climate change.

Researchers at the Oxford Martin Programme on the Future of Food have found that the economic benefit gained from the reduction in greenhouse gas emissions caused by a shift away from diets reliant on animal products could be as high as $570 billion.

A

B

The **Oxford Martin Programme on the Future of Food** connects research from different disciplines to help create a healthy and sustainable global food system.

Monoculture is when vast tracts of land are used to grow single crops, as has developed under industrial agriculture.

Dragging, also known as bottom trawling, refers to dragging a large weighted net along the ocean floor. The method scoops up everything in its path, leads to a lot of by-catch and causes damage to the ocean bed itself.

C

Results are difficult to predict, though, because the outcome varies according to how an animal-free food system would be set up. Would animal manure be replaced by plant-based fertilizer methods or synthetic ones, the production of which creates its own greenhouse gases? What kind of changes to imports and exports would occur?

Vast tracts of land used for monoculture, currently growing the grains needed to feed animals, could be dedicated to crops for people, thereby creating greater food resources on less land. The food available for humans would increase by a conservative estimate of 23% (factoring in the loss of food from meat and other animal products). However, one variable that is difficult to calculate in this equation is how much of the land is suitable for growing crops other than grains, because a vegan world would need a wide range of plant-based foods for optimum nutrition.

The effects of a shift to veganism would affect oceans positively. Overfished populations would have a chance to restore themselves. Habitats damaged by ocean floor dragging and other destructive methods could recover.

The oceans, which are warming and becoming increasingly acidic because of climate change, would also benefit from the reduction in greenhouse gases. A decrease in global warming, or at least the pace of it, would be good for the 70% of Earth's surface that is ocean.

A   Thick coats and ample layers of fat make it easy for polar bears to survive harsh Arctic weather, but warming temperatures and melting ice are cutting them off from the seals that are their main source of food, leading to widespread weight loss among the bears and threatening their survival as a species.

B   A satirical poke at the fast food giant Burger King, by Johnny Saraiva in 2010. The high amounts of fat, cholesterol and sodium found in many fast food burgers pose a risk to our cardiovascular health.

Warmer oceans, in turn, affect the weather. They cause less rain in most sub-tropical areas and more rainfall in many temperate mid-latitude regions, thereby impacting what can be grown where. And for each degree the oceans climb up the thermometer, severe hurricanes increase by 25 to 30%. In addition, warmer ocean water means more melting glaciers and polar ice, which leads to rising sea levels. A UN report released in 2018 by the Intergovernmental Panel on Climate Change found that a single degree rise in global temperature would raise ocean levels by 2.3 m (7½ feet), a change that would leave vast swathes of low-lying land everywhere from Myanmar to Florida underwater and make seasonal storms even more destructive. A large-scale shift to veganism could, quite conceivably, slow down the pace of all these climate-driven ocean issues.

A

For individual humans, a vegan planet would likely be a healthier one. Less heart disease, fewer cases of type 2 diabetes, a possible decrease in cancer rates: it is all easily imaginable in a vegan world. Some researchers suggest that the shift would mean 8.1 million fewer avoidable deaths per year.

Consideration should also be given to the improved quality of life for people who would avoid suffering from chronic diseases or conditions. Indeed, a reduction in lifestyle-related diseases would mean less pressure on health care systems and possible savings of between $700 and $1,000 billion in health care costs and lost working days. Some estimates put the value of the reduced risk of dying as between 9 and 13% of the global GDP, which would be $20 to $30 trillion.

A European dairy farmers spray milk at police officers during a demonstration outside the European Parliament in Brussels in 2012. They are protesting a cut in milk prices that they believe challenges the viability of the industry.
B During a similar demonstration in 2016 – this time against price cuts for meat and dairy – farmers blow straw at riot police from a mechanical spreader at the entrance to a Carrefour supermarket in Le Mans, France.
C European Milk Board representatives spray and burn milk powder outside a meeting of the EU agriculture ministers in Brussels, Belgium, in 2017. They are protesting against the sale of intervention milk powder and demanding a fair milk policy.

We must acknowledge, though, the fact that we get more from livestock than food. Farm animals recycle more than 43.2 billion kilograms (48 million tons) of food that is inedible to humans, including agricultural waste such as corn stalks, food waste such as potato peelings, fibre-processing by-products and distillery waste. Animals can eat these waste products and convert them into human food, pet food and industrial products, as well as 4 billion kilograms (4.4 million tons) of nitrogen fertilizer in the form of their own waste.

This brings us to the question of pets. Do they fit into a vegan lifestyle? On a philosophical level, if veganism is against any exploitation of animals, pets are not vegan. That said, most people who adopt a vegan lifestyle for animal welfare reasons love animals and often have pets. So the question is, can pets become vegan? Is an animal-free diet healthy for cats and dogs, for example? Even though they are carnivores, dogs can be kept healthy on a carefully regulated vegan diet. So, the development of varied vegan dog foods could solve this issue. Cats face a few more challenges, including the inability to process vitamin D2, which is the vitamin D found in plants, as opposed to vitamin D3, which is found in animals. Like humans, dogs can process D2 to some degree, although both cats and dogs are unable to process vitamin D from sunshine the way humans can. Cats also need higher levels of taurine, and can face heart and vision problems without it.

On the human front, a vegan planet would mean that meat producers, cheese makers and fishermen would lose their jobs. Entire industries would collapse.

In Britain, more than 315,000 people work directly in agricultural livestock. In France, livestock accounts for half of all agricultural income, the total of which was more than $132 billion in 2012. In Brazil, beef production alone accounts for 360,000 direct jobs and $13.7 billion in exports. The US livestock industry employs 1.6 million people and accounts for $31.8 billion in exports.

c

While a nutritionally sound vegan diet is entirely possible on an individual level, the scaling-up that would be necessary to cater for an entire population would be quite a challenge.

When animals convert certain energy-dense but micronutrient-poor foods, such as grass and grains, into muscle or milk or eggs, these foods become more micronutrient dense. It is one thing for a small percentage of the population to seek out micronutrients in other ways, but large economic and social changes would be needed to meet the requirements of the entire population.

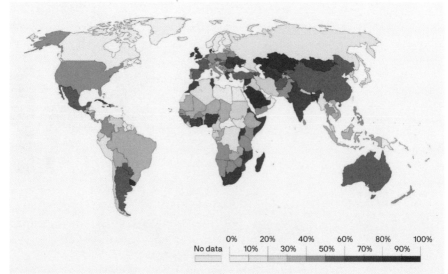

| No data | 0% | 20% | 40% | 60% | 80% | 100% |
| | 10% | 30% | 50% | 70% | 90% | |

A

Models of animal-free diets based on current eating patterns and budget tend to find an overall deficiency in vitamins B12, D, E and K, as well as in calcium and essential fatty acids. That said, current diets that include meat are deficient, on a population level, in calcium and vitamins D, E and K. It is no surprise that B12 and essential fatty acids are the most problematic: they are most commonly and easily obtained from animal sources.

A   This map shows the percentage of arable land in different countries around the world that is devoted to permanent agricultural use, either planted with crops or used for grazing.

B   Although many fruits and vegetables are already grown and much land is already under agricultural use, a shift to an all-vegan planet would require a dramatic change in how that land is used and what crops were planted for everyone to have access to a healthful diet.

Again, this does not mean that a vegan diet will have these deficiencies, just that the current system does not produce enough of the kinds of foods that we need to meet these nutritional requirements. Land use adjustments would be necessary in order to grow the right range of foods in sufficient quantities for proper nutrition for large populations. It is worth noting that current land use in many countries does not align with nutrition guidelines either. There are not enough fruits and vegetables grown and available in stores in Britain or the USA, for example, for everyone to buy and eat five servings a day as recommended.

A

B

Cost is another factor that affects people getting proper nutrition. In many countries, more nutritious foods tend to be more expensive than less nutritious foods. For example, in the USA in 2008, 100 calories of broccoli cost $1.93, while 100 calories of potato chips, with significantly fewer micronutrients and less dietary fibre, was just 33 cents; 100 calories of vitamin A-laden baby carrots was $2.50, whereas the same amount of candy was 39 cents.

As Michael Pollan, author of *The Omnivore's Dilemma* (2006), points out: 'The more a food is processed, the more profitable it gets.' It is not that a vegan planet would not have plenty of processed food, or that we often lack essential nutrients in our current omnivorous society, but rather that a vegan world does not necessarily solve the economic divide that exists

C

A   A policeman patrols the
    opening ceremony for a
    new McDonald's in Beijing
    in 2007. McDonald's
    opened its first restaurant
    in mainland China in 1990.
    By 2017, it operated more
    than 2,500 restaurants
    there, with plans to almost
    double that by 2022.
B   A Turkish doner kebab is
    an example of traditional
    food beloved both within
    and beyond its own culture;
    completely abandoning such
    dishes is a major impediment
    to an all-vegan planet.
C   The stalls selling deep fried
    food are part and parcel
    of the Utah State Fair.
    No matter how nutritionally
    disastrous these foods are,
    they remain celebrated and
    craved by lots of people.

between nutrient-rich and nutrient-poor foods. And vegans have a heightened need for nutrient-rich diets.

Perhaps the least predictable and the most interesting aspect of a vegan planet would be cultural. What we eat shapes not only our meals, but also trade patterns, social practices and even cultural beliefs.

Replacing the Christmas roast with a mushroom bake or stuffed squash is easy enough in terms of something to eat, but how long would it take for such a meal to 'feel like Christmas' for some people? What does a turkey-less Thanksgiving taste like? For occasions when the food is symbolic of more than the holiday and tradition itself, such as the lamb shank on a Seder plate for Passover or a whole fish for lunar New Year, some people will be more open to creative substitutions than others. Anthropologists may point to the inherent dynamism built into social practices: what is tradition to one generation may be unrecognizable three generations later.

Smoking rates remained around 44% for adults in the US from the 1940s into the 1970s. As rates have decreased to 16% in 2018, smoking has gone from a norm in offices and public places to something few tolerate. Could the same tipping point happen with meat eating? And do we want it to?

A Inupiat hunters harvest a whale in Utqiaġvik, Alaska (formerly known as Barrow). The meat from a single whale will feed the community through the winter and connects people to their cultural traditions and way of life.

B Whaling is big, community work – 150 people travelled three hours by snowmobile from Utqiaġvik, Alaska, to help butcher a Greenland right, or bowhead, whale.

Some cultures have developed animal-intensive diets for reasons of climate. What does a vegan Inuit or a vegan Maasai look like? How does veganism work in regions with short growing seasons? What happens in cultures where animal products are part and parcel of everyday life?

A

Inuit and Yupik have long survived on a high animal product diet of seal, walrus, whale, polar bear, caribou, birds, eggs and a wide variety of fish. All this meat and fish is augmented with wild berries, tubers, edible grasses and seaweed when available, but the vast majority of the traditional diet has been hunted rather than gathered.

Other people in climates with limited opportunity to develop agriculture, or with extremely short growing seasons, have diets that are traditionally high in meat, dairy and eggs. Not all of these population groups show ill effects from such a diet. Lots of paradoxes, including the Inuit paradox, exist, wherein a diet that appears unhealthy does not generate the presumed heart disease, high blood pressure and type 2 diabetes nutritionists would predict. In the case of Inuit, the high quotient of raw or frozen meat, along with lightly fermented meat (a process that creates higher levels of carbohydrates), seems to be a magical combination.

Inuit are indigenous people in the Arctic and sub-Arctic areas of Alaska, Canada and Greenland.

Maasai, meaning 'people who speak Maa', are an ethnic group in East Africa.

Yupik are indigenous people in the Arctic and sub-Arctic areas of Alaska and Eastern Russia.

B

The traditional Maasai diet is made of the milk, blood and meat – often raw meat – of the cattle they raise. Some Maasai almost never touch fruit or vegetables; others eat small amounts of them. As with the Inuit and Yupik, few negative health concerns seem to result. High activity levels in all groups have been cited as possible mitigating factors.

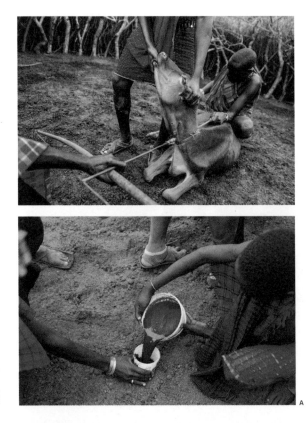

A	Masaai warriors slaughter a cow, draining its blood to make a traditional and highly sustaining drink of blood and milk. Raising cattle and eating this high-protein diet is so much a part of Masaai culture, it is clear that becoming vegan would completely upend their identity.

B	Founded in 1888, Katz's Delicatessen on Houston Street in New York, photographed here by Thomas Hoepker (1986), is famous for its traditional Jewish offerings, including pastrami, corned beef and smoked salmon – not to mention beef hot dogs, latkes with sour cream and matzo ball soup in rich chicken broth.

A

In any case, these are entire people and cultures built around hunting and eating animals. What happens, not only economically but also culturally if they need to import other food, if those practices cease to exist? Will they or can they be replaced? Or is it impossible to maintain an identity that was centuries or even millennia in the making if such a fundamental shift takes place?

All things considered, an all-vegan planet has much to offer.

It would almost certainly be greener, more sustainable and healthier for most people. But it might also seem to be a planet with less variety. Healthier in ways big and small, yes, but there is a legitimate question about how socially and psychologically sustainable – how genuinely human – it would be.

Conclusion

So, should we all be vegan? All evidence points to a qualified 'yes'.

For our personal health, animal welfare, environmental concerns and a sustainable food system, a human diet that is plant-centric solves a growing number of problems.

A   Vegetarian restaurants such as The Butcher's Daughter in New York and Los Angeles offer diners numerous plant-based options from what they call their 'vegetable slaughterhouse', where they 'chop, fillet and carve fresh produce'.

B   By Chloe, with branches in New York, Boston, Los Angeles and London, offers diners vegan takes on American diner favourites, such as burgers and fries, as well as vegan frozen treats instead of traditional shakes and malts.

However, given the fact that meat symbolizes abundance and cele-bration in many cultures, and the ability of animals to convert foods that are otherwise inedible to humans and make use of land that is otherwise unproductive – not to mention many people craving meat – it seems unlikely that a full switch to veganism will happen soon.

A

Plant-centric eating is a push against the Western tradition of putting meat at the centre of the plate. Instead, plant-based foods such as grains, legumes and vegetables are considered first, with animal products being used for highlighting flavour or texture, rather than as the main event of a meal.

But complete change – an all-vegan planet – is not needed to reap some, if not most, of the benefits of plant-based foods. People can harness the benefits of plant-centrism and positively affect the food system by making incremental changes.

Fewer people eating animal products, either full-time or for a day or more a week, would make for considerable change. Fewer animals to look after should mean that they could be raised according to the highest humane, sustainable and organic standards, in ways that allow them to express their natural behaviours, and that are not detrimental – are even helpful – to the environment. Consequently, their meat would be more nutritious, as a result of their improved diet and increased exercise, and their manure would provide a rich fertilizer for the plants that would form the bulk of our diet.

A

Chickens, both broilers and layers, could be pasture-raised. They could spend a portion of their time out of doors, not just in name but in spirit: hunting and pecking and scratching on meadow and pasture. They would then lay eggs full of the vitamins and minerals – and brilliantly coloured yolks – that come with a varied, natural diet, and produce meat created from a healthy diet and exercise, not Frankenstein-like breeding. Similarly, pigs could move back out of doors, nurse their piglets and wallow in mud to cool down. They could be fed a varied, nutritious omnivorous diet and produce flavourful, antibiotic-free meat.

A   Chickens at Polyface Farm in Swoope, Virginia, live outdoors during the day and in safe hen houses with perches at night. They are able to live as chickens would naturally: scratching and pecking for a varied diet and establishing pecking orders that keep the flock socially stable.

B   The improvement of school lunches in Britain and the USA has focused on getting fresh fruits and vegetables onto students' trays in place of highly processed foods.

Cattle could return to being entirely grass-fed, with nary a grain or feedlot in sight. Their grazing could be well managed and regenerative, improving the soil on which they graze instead of destroying it. As a result, their meat would be full of naturally occurring fatty acids to offset the cholesterol and saturated fat it contains, and still provide an impressive source of protein, iron and vitamin B12. Beef could go back to being something that is eaten occasionally, for celebration.

Diets featuring more plants and less meat would lead to health improvements even if everyone did not go completely or strictly vegan. Indeed, there are many possible models for ways of eating that harness some of the benefits of veganism without a wholesale rejection of all animal products. Some studies estimate the death rate would decrease by 10 to 15% if people simply did not eat red meat.

Such changes can also have environmental impact. In 2019, a study in *The Lancet* promoted the 'planetary health diet' to decrease diabetes, stroke and heart disease, as well as to mitigate environmental damage. The diet includes a dramatic reduction in red meat, sugar and processed foods while increasing whole grains, fruits, vegetables, nuts and legumes. Although far from vegan – the diet places importance on eating dairy, eggs, poultry and seafood – it shows that great health and environmental benefits promised by many vegan advocates can be realized by adopting diets that aren't 'all or nothing'.

Meatless Mondays is a prime example of a simple step towards eating less meat. The idea began in the USA in 2003 as a marketing initiative in cooperation with the Johns Hopkins Bloomberg School of Public Health to encourage people to avoid eating meat at least one day per week. Similar efforts now exist around the world to reduce the consumption of meat for environmental and public health reasons.

B

Many contemporary diet trends work on the notion of 'cheat days', wherein a fairly strict diet is followed for five or six days a week, leaving a day or two to be more flexible. Veganism could follow suit. The Duchess of Sussex has said that she eats vegan during the week and then has 'a little bit more flexibility with what I dig into on the weekends'. In a similar vein, Mark Bittman's book *VB6: Eat Vegan Before 6:00* (2013) outlines how to concentrate on ridding two out of three meals per day of animal products.

A Beyoncé's sweatshirt in her 2014 video for the song '7/11' both reflected and fuelled the millennial craze for kale, as sales of the previously little-known vegetable soared.

B Byron Hamburger's 'flexitarian' burger is 70% meat and 30% mushroom. It is aimed at those trying to reduce their meat intake without cutting it out completely.

C The sensation created by the launch of the Gregg's vegan sausage roll in 2019 demonstrated the huge demand for tasty vegan alternatives to traditional foods.

A

B

C

Beyoncé, an outspoken advocate of plant-based eating, admits that she is not always vegan. She adopts veganism when preparing for tours, and with her husband, Jay-Z, promotes a 22-day nutrition programme that is vegan. She says her vegan stints help her to make better, more thoughtful choices all the time. Naturally, many people find a complete rejection of meat, much less all animal products, difficult to maintain. Russell Brand and Venus Williams are both well-known vegans who admit that it is sometimes tough for them to stick to the diet, but they do their best.

Cheat days are set days on which people 'cheat' on their diets as part of the regime. The concept was popularized by Tim Ferriss's *The 4-Hour Body* (2010). Versions of it show up in many diets that vary the amount eaten on different days, such as the 5:2 diet.

Albert Einstein (1879–1955) was a theoretical physicist who developed the theory of relativity, a cornerstone of modern physics.

Even Albert Einstein, who touted the merits of being meat-free did not always follow through on it, despite having been a long-term sympathizer of the cause. 'Although I have been prevented by outward circumstances from observing a strictly vegetarian diet, I have long been an adherent to the cause in principle,' he wrote in 1930. 'Besides agreeing with the aims of vegetarianism for aesthetic and moral reasons, it is my view that a vegetarian manner of living by its purely physical effect on the human temperament would most beneficially influence the lot of mankind.'

A

As we have explored, for its purely physical effect veganism may well be the best choice, but humans are not only physical. We are social and cultural and psychological and culinary. 'Tell me what you eat,' wrote the early 19th-century French writer and gastronome Jean Anthelme Brillat-Savarin, 'and I'll tell you what you are.'

For this reason, veganism may be too much for many people, no matter how plentiful its benefits. Luckily, as with so many things, engaging with the benefits of a vegan lifestyle can take place on a continuum. It need not be all or nothing.

B

According to the United States Department of Agriculture, the number of farmers' markets in the USA doubled between 2006 and 2016. Bountiful markets are vibrant advertisements for better diets. The sheer variety of colours and flavours on offer, along with the opportunity to converse with the people who grow the food, can lead visitors to buy and cook more fresh produce, a major factor in improving diets overall.

While adopting vegan diets on a global scale would avoid 8.1 million deaths by 2050, a global vegetarian diet would prevent 7.3 million deaths, and diets that merely feature less meat would avoid 5.1 million. Similarly, while vegan diets would reduce greenhouse gas emissions by 70%, vegetarian diets would bring them down by 63%, and less meat-intensive eating could reduce them by 29%. Yes, veganism wins, but other options make a difference and might be more attainable.

Let us not make the perfect the enemy of the good. Any steps we take towards healthier diets and a more sustainable food system with fewer environmental impacts are going in the right direction.

Further Reading

Adams, C. J., *The Sexual Politics of Meat — 25th Anniversary Edition: A Feminist-Vegetarian Critical Theory* (London: Bloomsbury Academic, 2015)

The Animals Film, directed by M. Alaux and V. Schonfeld, Beyond the Frame Ltd, 1981

Campbell, T. C. and Campbell, T. M. II, *The China Study: Revised and Expanded Edition: The Most Comprehensive Study of Nutrition Ever Conducted and the Startling Implications for Diet, Weight Loss, and Long-Term Health* (Dallas: Benbella Books, 2016)

Clarke, E., *The Little Book of Veganism* (Chichester: Summersdale, 2015)

Davis, A., *Let's Eat Well to Keep Fit* (San Diego, CA: Harcourt, Brace and Company, 1954)

Davis, B. and Melina, V., *Becoming Vegan: The Complete Reference to Plant Nutrition* (Summertown: Book Pub Co, 2014)

Davis, G., *Proteinaholic: How Our Obsession With Meat Is Killing Us and What We Can Do About It* (New York: HarperOne, 2016)

Dawn, K., *Thanking the Monkey: Rethinking the Way We Treat Animals* (New York: William Murrow, 2014)

Estabrook, B., *Pig Tales: An Omnivore's Quest for Sustainable Meat* (New York, NY: W.W. Norton & Co, 2015)

Faruqi, S., *Project Animal Farm: An Accidental Journey into the Secret World of Farming and the Truth About our Food* (New York: Pegasus Books, 2016)

Foer, J. S., *Eating Animals* (New York: Little, Brown and Company, 2009)

Food Inc., directed by R. Kenner, Magnolia Pictures, 2008

Forks Over Knives, directed by L. Fulkerson, Monica Beach Media, 2011

Genoways, T., *The Chain: Farm, Factory, and the Fate of Our Food* (New York: HaperCollins, 2015)

Gregory, J., *Of Victorians and Vegetarians: The Vegetarian Movement in Nineteenth-Century Britain* (London: Tauris Academic Studies, 2006)

Hamilton, L., 'The Quinoa Quarrel', *Harper's Magazine*, May 2014

An Inconvenient Truth, directed by D. Guggenheim, Lawrence Bender Productions, 2006

Joy, M., *Why We Love Dogs, Eat Pigs, and Wear Cows* (Berkeley: Conari Press, 2011)

Kirby, D., *Animal Factory: The Looming Threat of Industrial Pig, Dairy, and Poultry Farms to Humans and the Environment* (New York: St. Martin's Griffin, 2011)

Lappé, A., *Diet for a Hot Planet: The Climate Crisis at the End of Your Fork and What You Can Do About It* (New York: Bloombury USA, 2011)

Lappé, F. M., *Diet for a Small Planet*, 20th anniversary edition (New York: Ballantine, 1991)

Lappé, F. M. and Lappé, A., *Hope's Edge: The Next Diet for a Small Planet* (New York: TarcherPerigee, 2003)

Lindstrom, E. C., *The Skeptical Vegan: My Journey from Notorious Meat Eater to Tofu-Munching Vegan – A Survival Guide* (New York: Skyhorse Press, 2017)

Marcus, E., *Vegan: The New Ethics of Eating* (Itahca: McBooks Press, 2000)

McWilliams, J., *The Modern Savage: Our Unthinking Decision to Eat Animals* (New York: Thomas Dunne Books, 2015)

Ofei, M. and Ofei, M., *The Minimalist Vegan: A Simple Manifesto on Why to Live With Less Stuff and More Compassion* (Edenvale: The Minimalist Co Pty, 2017)

Pollan, M., *Cooked: The Natural History of Transformation* (New York: Penguin Books, 2013)

Pollan, M., *The Omnivore's Dilemma: A Natural History of Four Meals* (New York: Penguin Books, 2007)

Pollan, M., 'Power Steer', *The New York Times*, March 31 2002

Preese, R., *Sins of the Flesh: A History of Ethical Vegetarian Thought* (Vancouver: UBC Press, 2008)

Schlosser, E., *Fast Food Nation* (New York: Mariner Books, 2001)

Shelley, P. B., *A Vindication of a Natural Diet* (London: J. Callow, 1813)

Sinclair, U., *The Jungle* (London: 1906)

Singer, P., *Animal Liberation: The Definitive Classic of the Animal Movement*, 40th anniversary edition (New York, NY: Open Road Media, 2015)

Spencer, C., *The Heretic's Feast: A History of Vegetarianism* (Lebanon, NH: University Press of New England, 1995)

Stuart, T., *The Bloodless Revolution: A Cultural History of Vegetarianism from 1600 to Modern Times* (New York: W.W. Norton & Co, 2007)

Super Size Me, directed by Morgan Spurlock, The Con, Kathbur Pictures, and Studio on Hudsan, 2004

Taft, C., *Millennial Vegan: Tips for Navigating Relationships, Wellness, and Everyday Life as a Young Animal Advocate* (Boston: Vegan Publishers, 2017)

Tuttle, W., *The World Peace Diet, Tenth Anniversary Edition: Eating for Spiritual Health and Social Harmony* (Brooklyn: Lantern Books, 2016)

Walters, K. and Portmess, L., *Ethical Vegetarianism: From Pythagoras to Peter Singer* (Albany: SUNY press, 1999)

Picture Credits

Every effort has been made to locate and credit copyright holders of the material reproduced in this book. The author and publisher apologize for any omissions or errors, which can be corrected in future editions.

a = above, b = below,
c = centre, l = left, r = right

63 r C. Ortiz Rojas / NOAA
64 l Lisa Noble / Getty Images
64 r nik wheeler / Alamy Stock Photo
65 Sharp / Travel Channel / Kobal / REX / Shutterstock
66 Sweet Potato Soul, by Jenné Claiborne, sweetpotatosoul.com
67 David L. Ryan / The Boston Globe via Getty Images
68 a Evgeniy Salov / Alamy Stock Photo
68 b Patrick Pleul / DPA / PA Images
69 Planet Surf Camps
70 l Sophia Spring
70 r Alicia Grimshaw, About Time Magazine
71 l rawmanda.com
71 r Paris by Vegan, @parisbyvegan
72–3 Visions of America / UIG via Getty Images
74 Team Vinchay Running Club, teamvinchay.org
75 a Elena Schweitzer / Dreamstime.com
75 b Ziprashantzi / Dreamstime.com
76 Wellcome Collection, London
77 Temple of Seitan, templeofseitan.co.uk
78 Antonio Romero / Science Photo Library
79 l Victor de Schwanberg / Science Photo Library
79 r Lindsey Rose Johnson
80 Roger Ressmeyer / Corbis / VCG via Getty Images
81 dpa picture alliance / Alamy Stock Photo
82 Holger Hollemann / AFP / Getty Images
83 NeONBRAND, Sprouts Farmers Market
85 b imageBROKER / Alamy Stock Photo
86 StockFood Ltd. / Alamy Stock Photo
87 al, ar, bl Yulli's Brews
87 br Alternation Brewing Company 88 VCG via Getty Images

89 l Nigel Roddis / Bloomberg via Getty Images
89 r Simon Dawson / Bloomberg via Getty Images
90 Reuters / Robert Pratta
91 Reuters / Jo Yong-Hak
92 Gaz Oakley
93 Ugly Vegan
94 a Nicolas Asfouri / AFP / Getty Images
94 b Lynn Betts / U.S. Department of Agriculture, Natural Resources Conservation Service
95 a NASA
95 b Liu Jin / AFP / Getty Images
96 www.Huguenotfarm.com
97 Veronique de Viguerie / Getty Images
98 Stefan Jeremiah / REX / Shutterstock
99 Lisa Wiltse / Bloomberg via Getty Images
100–1 Yuri Smityuk / TASS via Getty Images
102 Martin Parr / Magnum Photos
103 Graph from MEAT ATLAS, published by the Heinrich Böll Foundation, Berlin, Germany, and Friends of the Earth Europe, Brussels, Belgium, 2014
104 Catskill Animal Sanctuary, Saugerties, N.Y.
105 SWNS
106 Bowhunting.com
107 Florent Vergnes / AFP / Getty Images
108 Yasuyoshi Chiba / AFP / Getty Images
109 Reuters / Nacho Doce
110 Eddie Jim / The Sydney Morning Herald and The Age Photos
111 Food and Agriculture Organization of the United Nations, Global Livestock Environmental Assessment Model (GLEAM), http: / / www.fao.org / gleam / results / en /. Reproduced with permission

112 a RGB Ventures / SuperStock / Alamy Stock Photo
112 b The Book Worm / Alamy Stock Photo
113 Andreas Solaro / AFP / Getty Images
114 Biosphoto / Alamy Stock Photo
115 Energy Kitchen
116 a Geert Vanden Wijngaert / AP / REX / Shutterstock
116 b Jean-Francois Monier / AFP / Getty Images
117 Stephanie Lecocq / EPA / REX / Shutterstock
118 ourworldindata.org / yields-and-land-use-in-agriculture (Source www.fao.org/faostat/en/#data)
119 Richard Kalvar / Magnum Photos
120 l Guang Niu / Getty Images
120 r batuhan toker / Alamy Stock Photo
121 Talyn Sherer, talynsherer.com
122–3 Richard Olsenius / National Geographic / Getty Images
124 a hadynyah / Getty Images
124 b Basia Kruszewska
125 Thomas Hoepker / Magnum Photos
126–7 Andreu Dalmau / EPA-EFE / REX / Shutterstock
128 Robert K. Chin – Storefronts / Alamy Stock Photo
129 Krista Schlueter
130 Jessica Reeder, jhfearless.com
131 U.S. Department of Agriculture
133 l GirlEatsWorld.co.uk
133 r Edd Dracott / PA Archive / PA Images
134 Photofusion / UIG via Getty Images
135 Dukas / UIG via Getty Images Shutterstock
135 a Banaras Khan / AFP / Getty Images
135 b Sabah Arar / AFP / Getty Images

Index

Acknowledgments:

All books are the result of extensive teamwork.
I owe a tremendous debt to Jane Laing, Tristan
de Lancey, Phoebe Lindsley and Isabel Jessop
at Thames & Hudson for the insight, expertise
and patience with a far-flung writer necessary
to produce this volume. A host of friends and
colleagues knowingly and unknowingly played
a part in this book, most notably Tara Duggan,
Clare Leschin-Hoar, Urvashi Rangan, and Kate
Washington. Lively debates about who eats
what and why are the least of the reasons my
gratitude to Steven Wolf and Ernest Wolf is,
as always, endless.